MathFlare

Name: _______________________

Class: ___________

Teacher: _______________________

<u>Introduction</u>

As parents and educators, we recognize the pivotal role mathematics plays in shaping a child's academic journey and future success. Yet, the path to mathematical proficiency can often seem daunting, fraught with challenges and complexities. That's where the transformative power of MathFlare Workbooks shine through, illuminating the way forward with clarity, precision, and purpose.

Introducing MathFlare Workbooks – a beacon of guidance, a testament to excellence, and a catalyst for achievement. Crafted with meticulous care and expertise, MathFlare Workbooks stand as paragons of educational excellence, designed to nurture young minds, ignite a passion for learning, and develop a deep-rooted understanding of mathematical concepts.

Picture this: your child eagerly delves into the pages of Mathflare Workbook, greeted by a step-by-step guide illuminated with vivid examples that demystify complex mathematical concepts. With each turn of the page, they embark on a journey of discovery, encountering thoughtfully curated practice questions that reinforce learning and hone problem-solving skills. And when they unveil the answers to those very questions, a sense of accomplishment blossoms within them – a tangible reward for their hard work and dedication.

But MathFlare Workbooks are more than just tools for learning; they are pathways to comprehension, fostering a deep-seated understanding of mathematical concepts through a sequential, logical flow. From fundamental principles to advanced problem-solving strategies, every chapter builds upon the last, ensuring a robust foundation upon which future knowledge can be constructed.

As parents, we yearn for nothing more than to see our children thrive, to witness the spark of inspiration ignited within them as they conquer academic challenges with confidence and poise. MathFlare Workbooks serve as partners in this noble endeavor, offering not just practice questions, but the keys to unlocking a world of opportunity.

And for teachers, MathFlare Workbooks stand as invaluable allies in the quest to cultivate mathematical proficiency in the classroom. With answers readily available, instructors can focus on guiding and nurturing their students, confident in the knowledge that MathFlare Workbooks provide a solid framework upon which to build.

In the pages of MathFlare Workbooks, we find not just the promise of academic excellence, but the seeds of a brighter tomorrow. So let us embrace the power of mathematics, let us champion the journey of learning, and let us pave the way for a generation of young minds poised to shape the world. With MathFlare Workbooks as our guide, the possibilities are infinite, and the future, bright.

Table of Contents

MathFlare
MATH
WORKBOOK
Grade 2
Step by Step Guide
and Essential Practice
with Answers
Addition
Subtraction
Multiplication
Place Value and
Expanded Notations
Geometry
MathFlare Publishing

MathFlare
MATH
WORKBOOK
Grade 2-3
Step by Step Guide
and Essential Practice
with Answers
Addition
Subtraction
Multiplication
and Division
Place Value and
Expanded Notations
Geometry
MathFlare Publishing

MathFlare
MATH
WORKBOOK
Grade 3
Step by Step Guide
and Essential Practice
with Answers
Multiplication
and Division
Decimals
Place Value and
Expanded Notations
Fractions
and Geometry
MathFlare Publishing

MathFlare
MATH
WORKBOOK
Grade 1
Step by Step Guide
and Essential Practice
with Answers
Counting and
Numbers
Addition and
Subtraction
Place Value and
Expanded
Notations
Understanding
Time
MathFlare Publishing

MathFlare
MATH
WORKBOOK
Grade 1-2
Step by Step Guide
and Essential Practice
with Answers
Counting and
Numbers
Addition and
Subtraction
Place Value and
Expanded
Notations
Understanding
Time
MathFlare Publishing

MathFlare
MATH
WORKBOOK
Grade 3-4
Step by Step Guide
and Essential Practice
with Answers
Addition
Subtraction
Multiplication
Division
Place Value and
Expanded
Notations
Fractions
and Geometry
MathFlare Publishing

MathFlare
MATH
WORKBOOK
Grade 4
Step by Step Guide
and Essential Practice
with Answers
Addition
Subtraction
Multiplication
Division
Place Value and
Expanded
Notations
Fractions
and Geometry
MathFlare Publishing

MathFlare
MATH
WORKBOOK
Grade 4-5
Step by Step Guide
and Essential Practice
with Answers
Multiplication
Division
Place Value and
Expanded
Notations
Fractions
and Geometry
Unit
Conversion
MathFlare Publishing

MathFlare
Grade 5
MATH WORKBOOK
Step by Step Guide and Essential Practice with Answers
Multiplication Division
Place Value and Expanded Notations
Fractions and Geometry
Unit Conversion
MathFlare Publishing

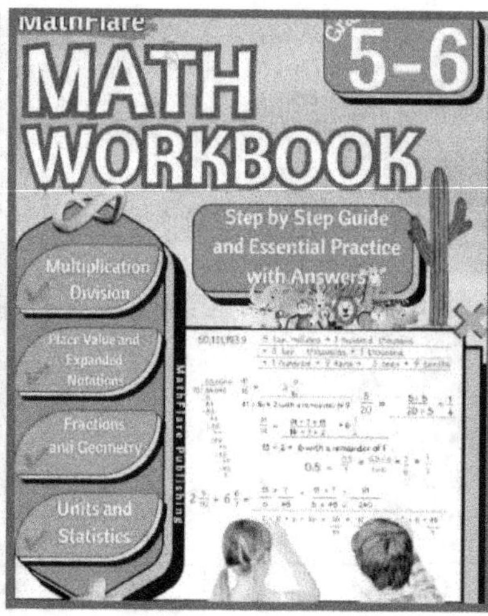
MathFlare
Grade 5-6
MATH WORKBOOK
Step by Step Guide and Essential Practice with Answers
Multiplication Division
Place Value and Expanded Notations
Fractions and Geometry
Units and Statistics
MathFlare Publishing

MathFlare
Grade 6
MATH WORKBOOK
Step by Step Guide and Essential Practice with Answers
Integers and Statistics
Arithmetic and Pre-Algebra
Fractions and Geometry
Ratio and Percentage
MathFlare Publishing

MathFlare
Grade 6-7
MATH WORKBOOK
Step by Step Guide and Essential Practice with Answers
Arithmetic and Pre-Algebra
Ratio, Percent Proportion
Geometry
Statistics
MathFlare Publishing

MathFlare
Grade 7
MATH WORKBOOK
Step by Step Guide and Essential Practice with Answers
Pre-Algebra
Ratio, Percent Proportion
Geometry
Statistics
MathFlare Publishing

MathFlare
Grade 7-8
MATH WORKBOOK
Step by Step Guide and Essential Practice with Answers
Pre-Algebra
Ratio, Percent Proportion
Geometry and Cartesian Plane
Statistics
MathFlare Publishing

MathFlare
Grade 8-9
MATH WORKBOOK
Step by Step Guide and Essential Practice with Answers
Pre-Algebra
Ratio, Proportion and Percentage
Linear Equations
Geometry and Cartesian Plane
MathFlare Publishing

MathFlare
Grade 8
MATH WORKBOOK
Step by Step Guide and Essential Practice with Answers
Pre-Algebra
Percentage
Linear Equations
Geometry
MathFlare Publishing

Chapter. 01

Addition and Subtraction

Addition with Regrouping

When we do addition, we combine numbers. But sometimes, when we're adding numbers, we might need to regroup. Regrouping means we have to move a number from one place to another, usually to the next column, to get the right answer.

For Example: Let's take an example of adding 533 and 579 together:

$$
\begin{array}{r}
5\ 3\ 3 \\
+\ 5\ 7\ 9 \\
\hline
\end{array}
$$

First, we start by adding the digits in the ones place: 3 + 9 = 12. We write down the 2 in the ones place and carry over the 1 to the tens place.

$$
\begin{array}{r}
1 \\
5\ 3\ 3 \\
+\ 5\ 7\ 9 \\
\hline
2
\end{array}
$$

Now, we add the digits in the tens place, along with the carry-over: 2 + 8 + 1 = 11. We write down the 1 in the tens place and carry over the 1 to the hundreds place.

$$
\begin{array}{r}
1\ 1 \\
5\ 2\ 2 \\
+\ 5\ 8\ 9 \\
\hline
1\ 2
\end{array}
$$

Now, we add the digits in the hundreds place, along with the carry-over: 5 + 5 + 1 = 11. We write down the 1 in the tens place and carry over the 1 to the hundreds place.

$$
\begin{array}{r}
1\ 1 \\
5\ 2\ 2 \\
+\ 5\ 8\ 9 \\
\hline
1\ 1\ 1\ 2
\end{array}
$$

This process of carrying over helps us accurately add numbers, especially when they're larger.

Subtraction with Regrouping

Subtraction is a key math operation where we find the difference between two numbers. Sometimes, when we subtract, we might need to regroup, which means borrowing from the next column.

Let's take an example of subtracting 436 from 563:

First, we start by subtracting the digits in the ones place: 3 - 6.

Since 3 is less than 6, we need to regroup. We borrow 1 from the tens place, making it 5 tens instead of 6, and add it to the ones place.

So, 3 becomes 13, and then we subtract 6.

$$
\begin{array}{r}
5\ \ 6\ _1 3 \\
-\ 4\ 3\ 6 \\
\hline
7
\end{array}
$$

Now, we subtract the tens place digits: 5 - 3 = 2

$$
\begin{array}{r}
5 \\
5\ \ \cancel{6}\,_1 3 \\
-\ 4\ 3\ 6 \\
\hline
2\ 7
\end{array}
$$

Now, we subtract the hundreds place digits: 5 - 4 = 1

$$
\begin{array}{r}
5 \\
5\ \ \cancel{6}\ ^1 3 \\
-\ 4\ \ 3\ \ 6 \\
\hline
1\ \ 2\ \ 7
\end{array}
$$

This process of regrouping or borrowing helps us accurately subtract numbers, especially when the top digit is smaller than the bottom one.

Let's solve problems from exercises:

$$
\begin{array}{r}
793 \\
+\ 459 \\
\hline
1{,}252 \\
\hline
\end{array}
\qquad
\begin{array}{r}
523 \\
-\ 285 \\
\hline
238 \\
\hline
\end{array}
$$

Word Problems

Word problems are like little puzzles that help us use addition in real-life situations.

For instance:

1. Jake has 6 carrots. He gets 2 more carrots. How many carrots does he have now?

To find out how many carrots he has now, we add the number of carrots he started with (6) to the number of carrots he got (2).

So, we add 6 + 2, which equals 8. Jake now has 8 carrots in total!

2. Jake saved up 4 dollars to buy pencils. He spent 2 dollars on it. How much money does he have left?

To solve this problem, we need to start with the number of dollars Jake started with and subtract the number of dollars he spent on the pencils.

So, we subtract 2 from 4, which equals 2: Jake has 2 dollars left after buying the pencils.

We need to understand what the problem is asking and what information it provides. Then, we can use addition or subtraction, depending on whether we're combining or taking away objects, to find the answer.

Let's solve problems from exercises:

Alice rode a horse for 8 miles yesterday and 16 miles today. In total, how many miles did she ride?

$$\begin{array}{rl} 8 & \text{Alice rode 8 miles yesterday} \\ +\ 16 & \text{She rode 16 miles today} \\ \hline 24 & \text{She rode 24 miles in total} \end{array}$$

There are 2 calculators in a bag. Samantha took 2 calculators   out of the bag. How many calculators are still in the bag?

$$\begin{array}{rl} 2 & \text{there are 2 calculators in the bag} \\ -\ 2 & \text{Samantha took 2 calculators} \\ \hline 0 & \text{there are 0 calculators in the bag} \end{array}$$

Addition with Regrouping

Find the sum.

1) 793 + 459 __1,252__	2) 463 + 757 __1,220__	3) 711 + 799	4) 133 + 978
5) 334 + 789	6) 771 + 479	7) 84 + 687	8) 989 + 493
9) 385 + 839	10) 546 + 67	11) 113 + 997	12) 931 + 899
13) 947 + 988	14) 337 + 776	15) 721 + 789	16) 389 + 875
17) 484 + 888	18) 114 + 999	19) 163 + 979	20) 512 + 599

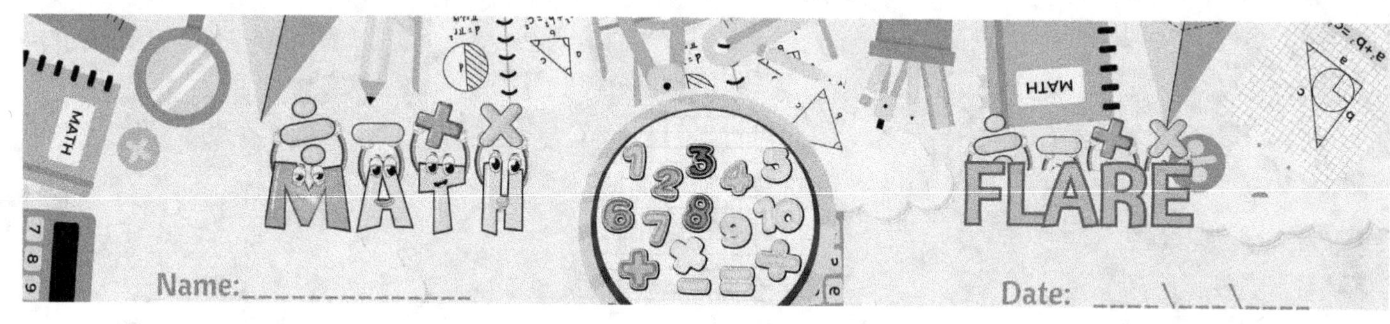

21) 589
+ 587
——

22) 349
+ 774
——

23) 441
+ 769
——

24) 843
+ 678
——

25) 823
+ 887
——

26) 41
+ 279
——

27) 883
+ 928
——

28) 312
+ 998
——

29) 528
+ 596
——

30) 817
+ 793
——

31) 924
+ 598
——

32) 216
+ 995
——

33) 171
+ 999
——

34) 991
+ 739
——

35) 569
+ 762
——

36) 331
+ 989
——

37) 327
+ 97
——

38) 458
+ 696
——

39) 499
+ 897
——

40) 457
+ 699
——

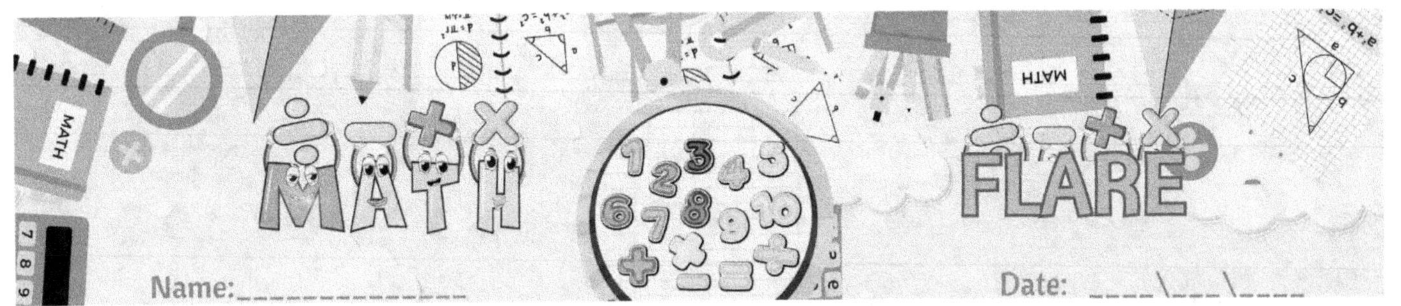

41) 116 + 998	42) 778 + 549	43) 125 + 988	44) 392 + 759
45) 83 + 168	46) 712 + 599	47) 962 + 759	48) 611 + 99
49) 372 + 989	50) 565 + 945	51) 518 + 694	52) 47 + 64
53) 851 + 469	54) 951 + 879	55) 471 + 789	56) 449 + 682
57) 111 + 999	58) 658 + 884	59) 755 + 676	60) 46 + 79

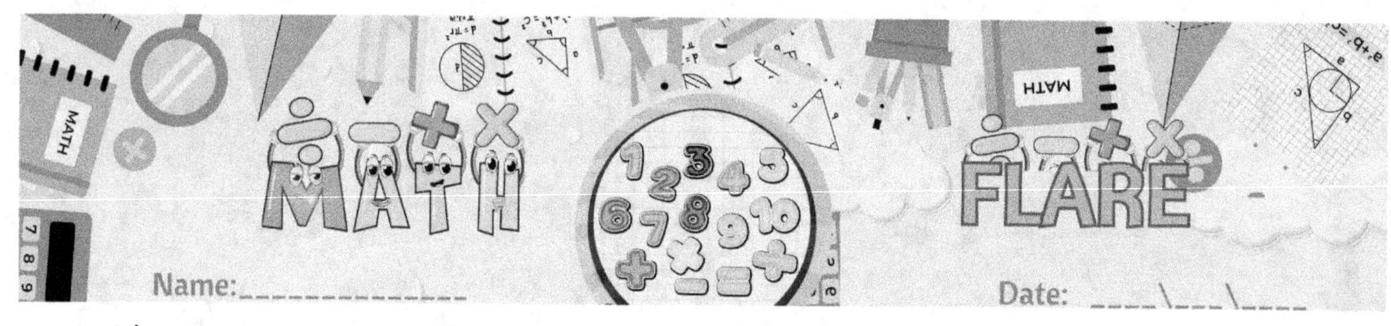

61) 115 + 996	62) 618 + 492	63) 59 + 774	64) 653 + 578
65) 411 + 699	66) 145 + 978	67) 633 + 598	68) 921 + 999
69) 676 + 785	70) 691 + 699	71) 162 + 988	72) 87 + 296
73) 719 + 391	74) 488 + 993	75) 93 + 478	76) 312 + 999
77) 135 + 987	78) 841 + 89	79) 527 + 685	80) 6 + 117

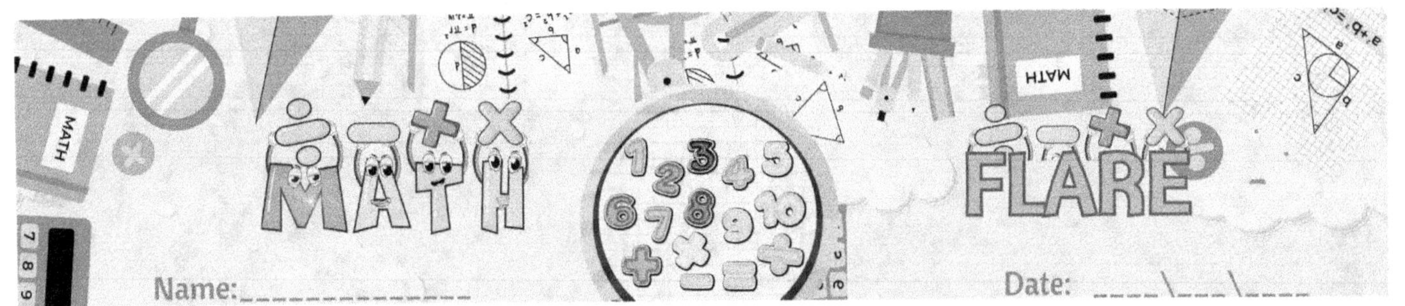

81) 774 + 378	82) 472 + 69	83) 643 + 997	84) 699 + 598
85) 451 + 699	86) 528 + 84	87) 986 + 347	88) 897 + 586
89) 351 + 889	90) 684 + 688	91) 247 + 67	92) 486 + 997
93) 186 + 927	94) 671 + 839	95) 436 + 97	96) 711 + 599
97) 925 + 788	98) 49 + 68	99) 653 + 598	100) 672 + 899

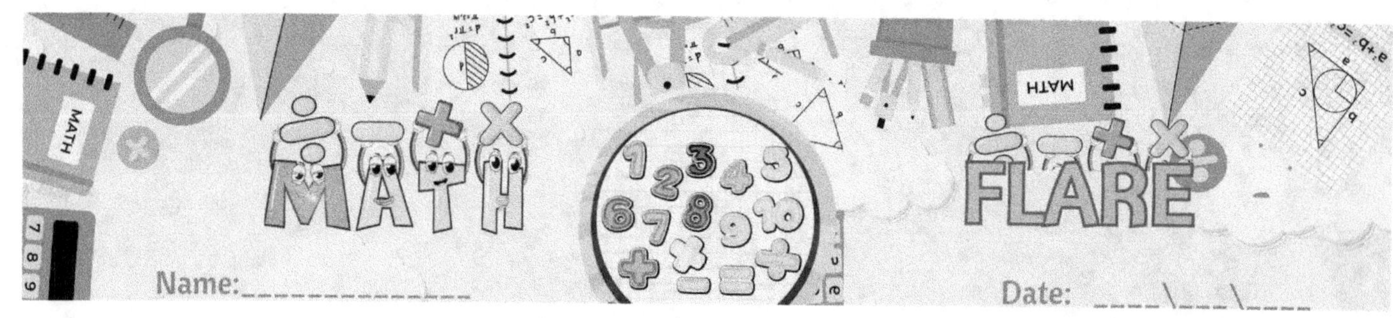

101) 145 + 996	102) 881 + 269	103) 611 + 499	104) 733 + 777
105) 961 + 369	106) 871 + 769	107) 887 + 478	108) 968 + 195
109) 944 + 576	110) 927 + 689	111) 261 + 899	112) 331 + 789
113) 422 + 699	114) 538 + 873	115) 669 + 95	116) 17 + 396
117) 915 + 98	118) 115 + 999	119) 741 + 399	120) 517 + 696

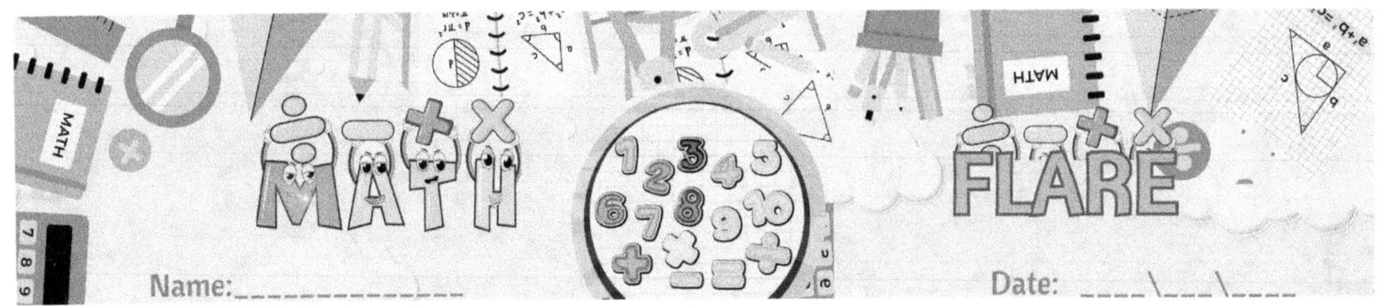

121) 116 + 997	122) 71 + 399	123) 713 + 799	124) 911 + 599
125) 51 + 469	126) 646 + 976	127) 963 + 578	128) 136 + 984
129) 931 + 299	130) 367 + 896	131) 718 + 493	132) 536 + 877
133) 311 + 899	134) 799 + 797	135) 365 + 898	136) 455 + 867
137) 58 + 552	138) 517 + 94	139) 427 + 997	140) 711 + 999

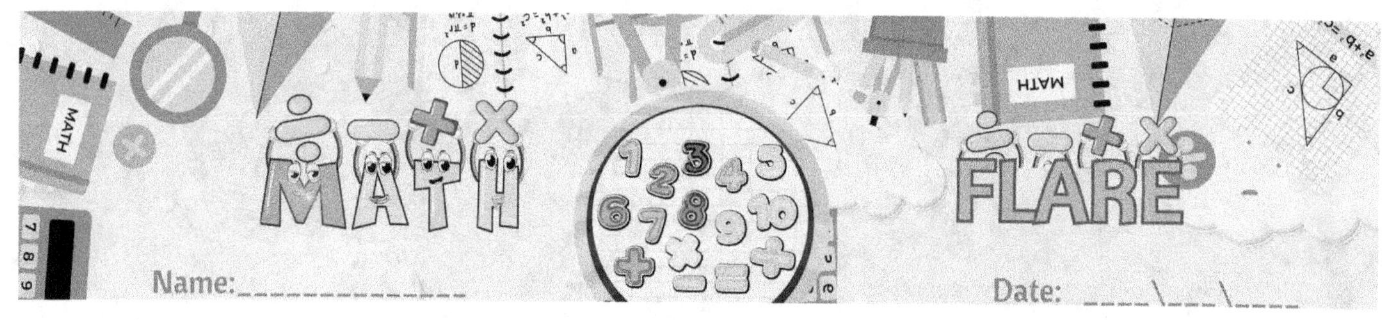

141) 219 + 997	142) 284 + 856	143) 449 + 988	144) 393 + 789
145) 955 + 768	146) 917 + 494	147) 32 + 89	148) 698 + 746
149) 696 + 954	150) 93 + 188	151) 411 + 899	152) 217 + 997
153) 6 + 107	154) 43 + 478	155) 27 + 197	156) 957 + 994
157) 585 + 955	158) 292 + 858	159) 117 + 997	160) 419 + 894

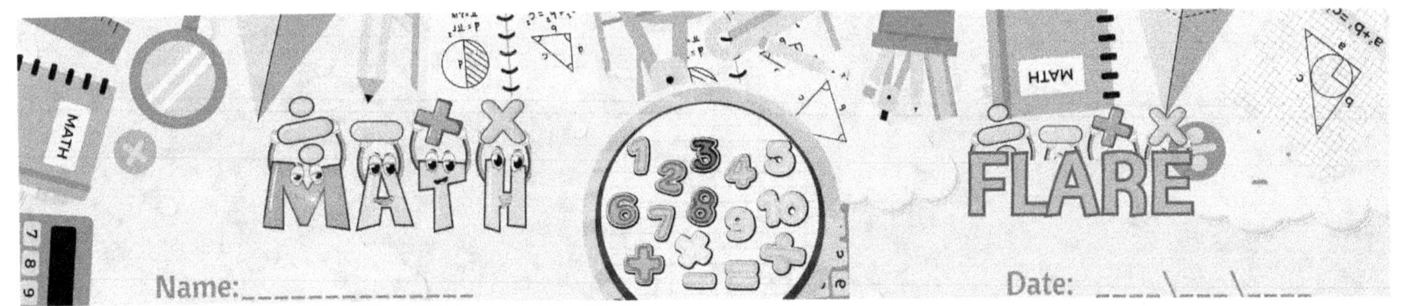

Name:____________________   Date: _____________

161) 123
    + 987
    ____

162) 843
    + 668
    ____

163) 223
    + 99
    ____

164) 516
    + 99
    ____

165) 814
    + 897
    ____

166) 334
    + 876
    ____

167) 845
    + 596
    ____

168) 811
    + 399
    ____

169) 761
    + 369
    ____

170) 876
    + 945
    ____

171) 357
    + 869
    ____

172) 774
    + 976
    ____

173) 859
    + 877
    ____

174) 724
    + 997
    ____

175) 591
    + 679
    ____

176) 785
    + 759
    ____

177)   66
    + 995
    ____

178) 262
    + 978
    ____

179) 698
    + 993
    ____

180) 583
    +   8
    ____

MathFlare - Math Workbook 2nd and 3rd Grade

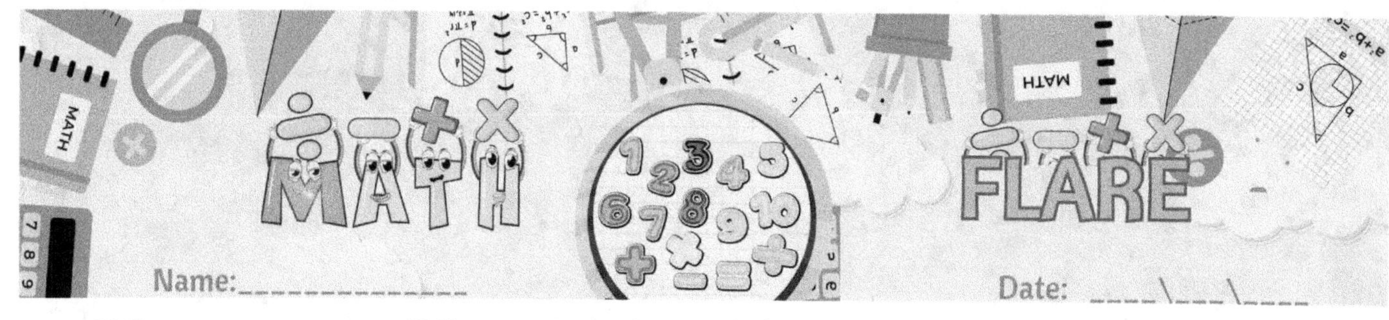

181) 639 + 687	182) 773 + 739	183) 151 + 69	184) 354 + 887
185) 991 + 759	186) 123 + 99	187) 518 + 993	188) 61 + 999
189) 861 + 369	190) 154 + 956	191) 318 + 897	192) 212 + 998
193) 439 + 897	194) 459 + 866	195) 845 + 489	196) 667 + 477
197) 767 + 875	198) 313 + 797	199) 77 + 47	200) 764 + 797

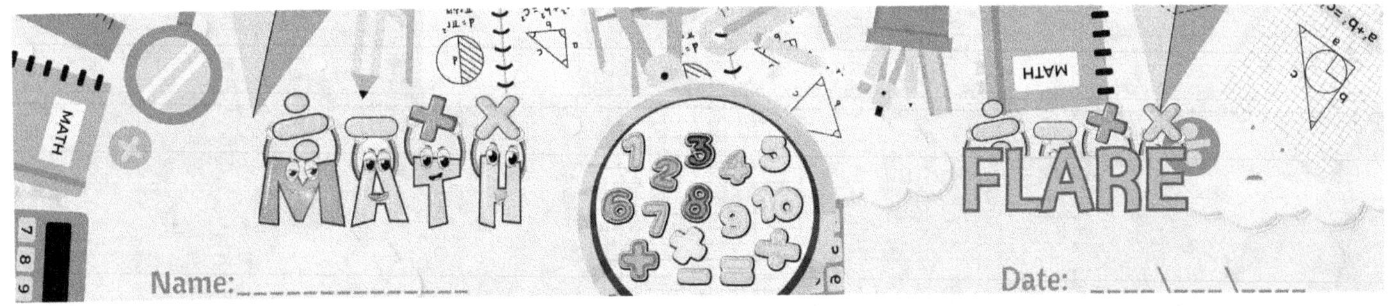

Subtraction with Regrouping

Find the difference.

1) 523
  − 285
  238

2) 957
  − 899
  58

3) 248
  − 179

4) 202
  − 179

5) 935
  − 258

6) 714
  − 278

7) 841
  − 794

8) 683
  − 597

9) 26
  − 19

10) 295
  − 6

11) 604
  − 339

12) 342
  − 274

13) 87
  − 79

14) 302
  − 198

15) 980
  − 897

16) 918
  − 759

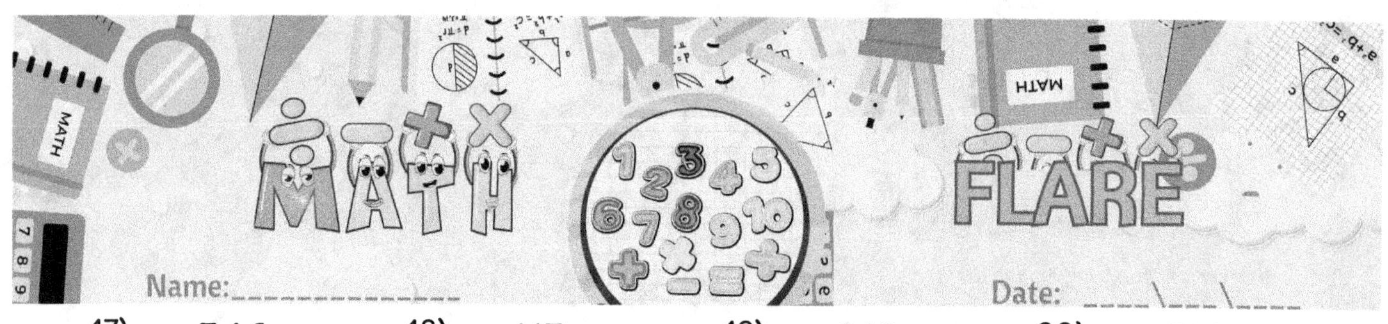

17) 546 − 197	18) 117 − 98	19) 910 − 341	20) 718 − 549
21) 935 − 568	22) 871 − 584	23) 475 − 199	24) 471 − 395
25) 283 − 195	26) 117 − 38	27) 747 − 568	28) 284 − 199
29) 187 − 98	30) 752 − 284	31) 415 − 237	32) 5 − 1
33) 450 − 363	34) 843 − 499	35) 828 − 749	36) 861 − 573

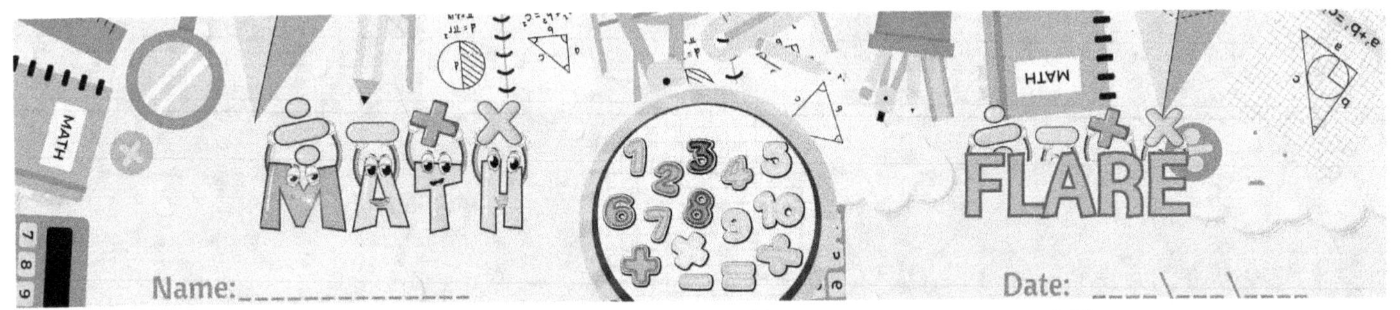

37) 91
   - 53

38) 80
   - 3

39) 676
   - 597

40) 328
   - 269

41) 540
   - 259

42) 440
   - 154

43) 813
   - 529

44) 73
   - 58

45) 163
   - 84

46) 584
   - 497

47) 622
   - 237

48) 308
   - 119

49) 571
   - 494

50) 230
   - 174

51) 436
   - 387

52) 986
   - 299

53) 670
   - 388

54) 178
   - 99

55) 672
   - 189

56) 300
   - 132

57) 828 − 789	58) 888 − 799	59) 131 − 86	60) 285 − 197
61) 823 − 45	62) 323 − 266	63) 320 − 35	64) 20 − 14
65) 266 − 198	66) 458 − 379	67) 536 − 489	68) 373 − 294
69) 484 − 97	70) 678 − 299	71) 573 − 495	72) 224 − 197
73) 841 − 189	74) 927 − 679	75) 583 − 297	76) 336 − 259

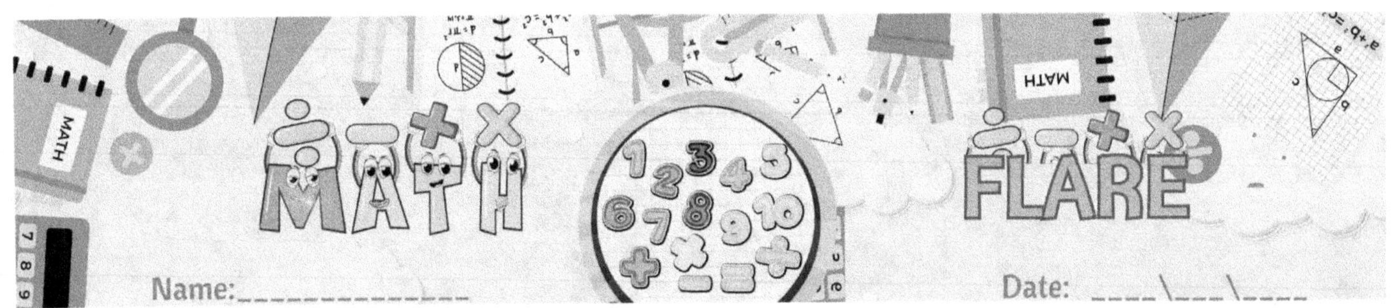

77) 671 − 386	78) 757 − 298	79) 564 − 175	80) 970 − 598
81) 455 − 266	82) 908 − 879	83) 706 − 348	84) 887 − 98
85) 572 − 83	86) 553 − 494	87) 977 − 888	88) 328 − 299
89) 926 − 377	90) 845 − 157	91) 180 − 92	92) 228 − 159
93) 478 − 289	94) 142 − 6	95) 980 − 896	96) 91 − 17

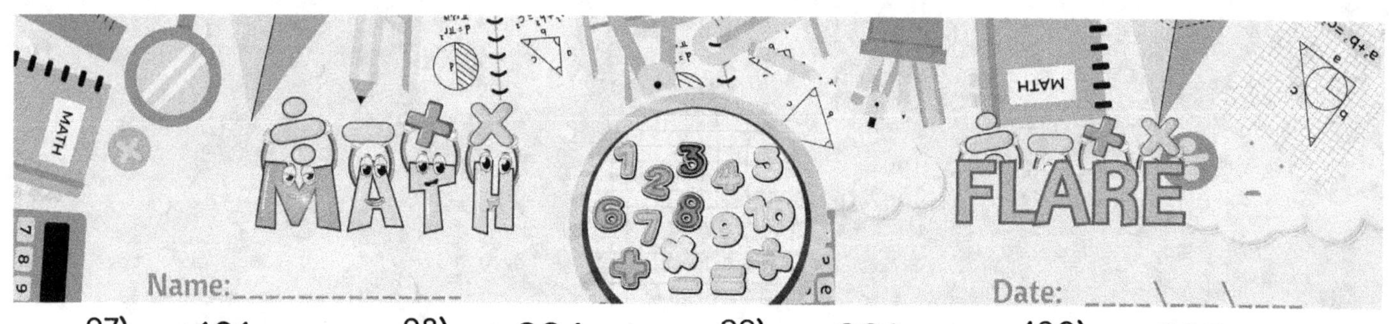

97)	98)	99)	100)
181 - 92	884 - 5	981 - 194	283 - 194

101)	102)	103)	104)
356 - 287	108 - 49	918 - 239	938 - 769

105)	106)	107)	108)
303 - 259	461 - 197	464 - 379	385 - 97

109)	110)	111)	112)
341 - 6	480 - 99	448 - 389	93 - 55

113)	114)	115)	116)
55 - 16	788 - 699	971 - 297	934 - 795

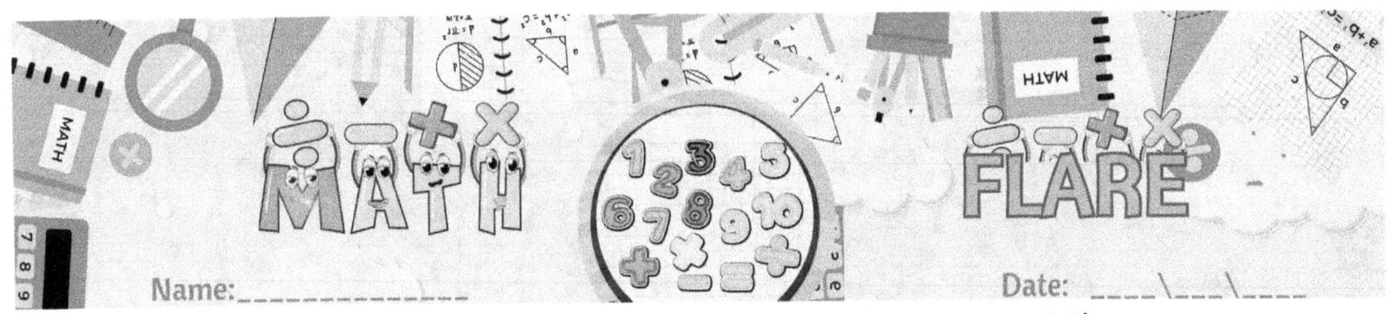

117)
$$\begin{array}{r} 33 \\ -\ 17 \\ \hline \end{array}$$

118)
$$\begin{array}{r} 912 \\ -\ 326 \\ \hline \end{array}$$

119)
$$\begin{array}{r} 235 \\ -\ 169 \\ \hline \end{array}$$

120)
$$\begin{array}{r} 976 \\ -\ 288 \\ \hline \end{array}$$

121)
$$\begin{array}{r} 604 \\ -\ 197 \\ \hline \end{array}$$

122)
$$\begin{array}{r} 704 \\ -\ 115 \\ \hline \end{array}$$

123)
$$\begin{array}{r} 526 \\ -\ 447 \\ \hline \end{array}$$

124)
$$\begin{array}{r} 711 \\ -\ 268 \\ \hline \end{array}$$

125)
$$\begin{array}{r} 730 \\ -\ 562 \\ \hline \end{array}$$

126)
$$\begin{array}{r} 765 \\ -\ 687 \\ \hline \end{array}$$

127)
$$\begin{array}{r} 686 \\ -\ 99 \\ \hline \end{array}$$

128)
$$\begin{array}{r} 7 \\ -\ 3 \\ \hline \end{array}$$

129)
$$\begin{array}{r} 753 \\ -\ 394 \\ \hline \end{array}$$

130)
$$\begin{array}{r} 385 \\ -\ 297 \\ \hline \end{array}$$

131)
$$\begin{array}{r} 457 \\ -\ 79 \\ \hline \end{array}$$

132)
$$\begin{array}{r} 844 \\ -\ 68 \\ \hline \end{array}$$

133)
$$\begin{array}{r} 888 \\ -\ 699 \\ \hline \end{array}$$

134)
$$\begin{array}{r} 308 \\ -\ 229 \\ \hline \end{array}$$

135)
$$\begin{array}{r} 882 \\ -\ 96 \\ \hline \end{array}$$

136)
$$\begin{array}{r} 878 \\ -\ 599 \\ \hline \end{array}$$

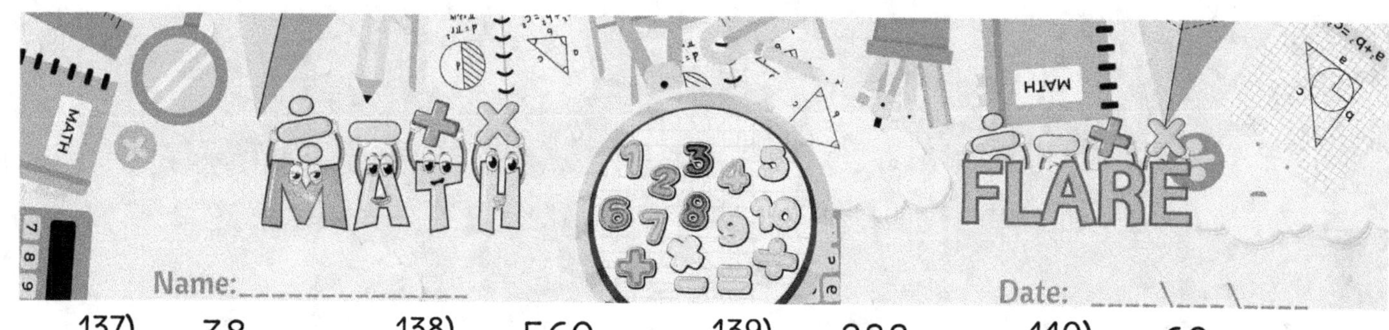

137)   38
      − 19
    ______

138)   560
      − 83
    ______

139)   288
      − 199
    ______

140)   60
      − 13
    ______

141)   568
      − 279
    ______

142)   134
      − 48
    ______

143)   658
      − 599
    ______

144)   76
      − 69
    ______

145)   486
      − 299
    ______

146)   582
      − 495
    ______

147)   304
      − 197
    ______

148)   766
      − 488
    ______

149)   481
      − 393
    ______

150)   358
      − 289
    ______

151)   643
      − 475
    ______

152)   485
      − 399
    ______

153)   881
      − 92
    ______

154)   940
      − 463
    ______

155)   670
      − 581
    ______

156)   277
      − 189
    ______

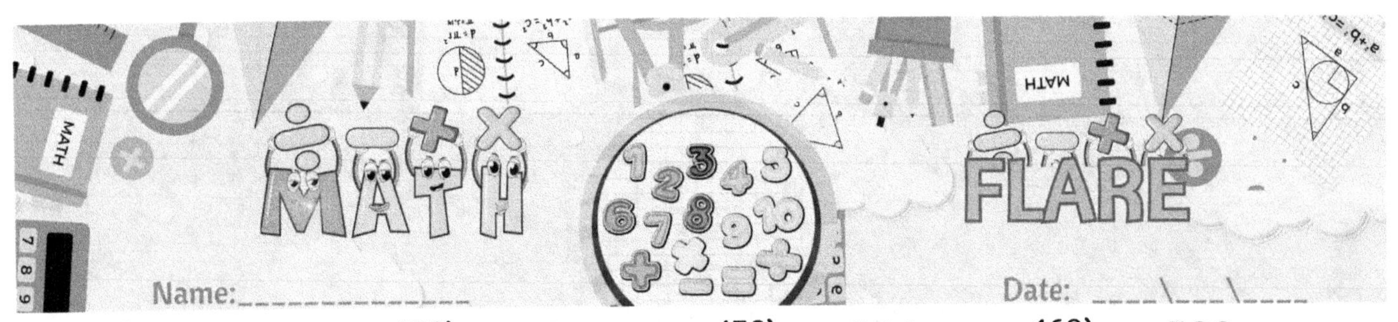

157) 463
  - 84
	158) 72
	  - 3
		159) 944
		  - 687
			160) 522
			  - 498

161) 626
  - 197
	162) 487
	  - 199
		163) 470
		  - 99
			164) 348
			  - 289

165) 483
  - 97
	166) 542
	  - 356
		167) 678
		  - 199
			168) 562
			  - 476

169) 938
  - 459
	170) 311
	  - 174
		171) 27
		  - 18
			172) 334
			  - 168

173) 371
  - 283
	174) 250
	  - 82
		175) 266
		  - 199
			176) 584
			  - 495

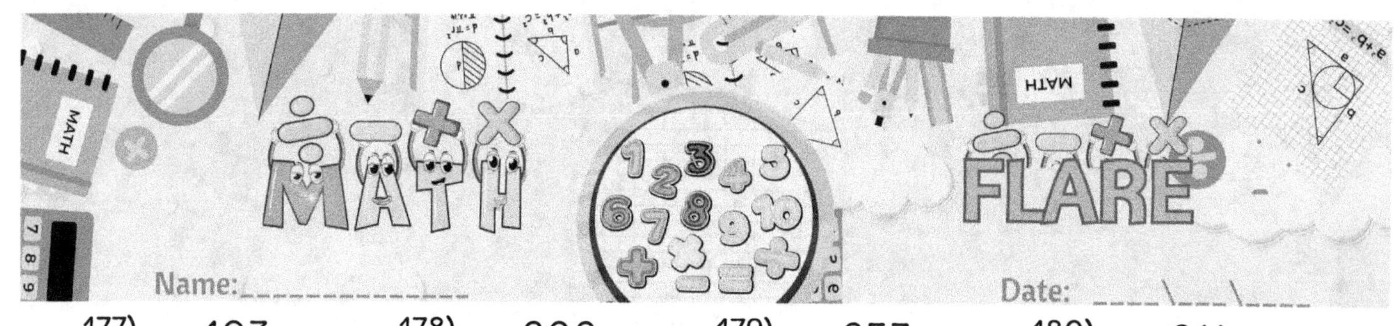

177) 103 − 36	178) 200 − 69	179) 253 − 76	180) 211 − 153
181) 664 − 188	182) 936 − 549	183) 444 − 279	184) 141 − 83
185) 620 − 151	186) 97 − 48	187) 433 − 345	188) 926 − 859
189) 970 − 886	190) 974 − 688	191) 917 − 299	192) 436 − 379
193) 463 − 199	194) 36 − 9	195) 578 − 489	196) 244 − 159

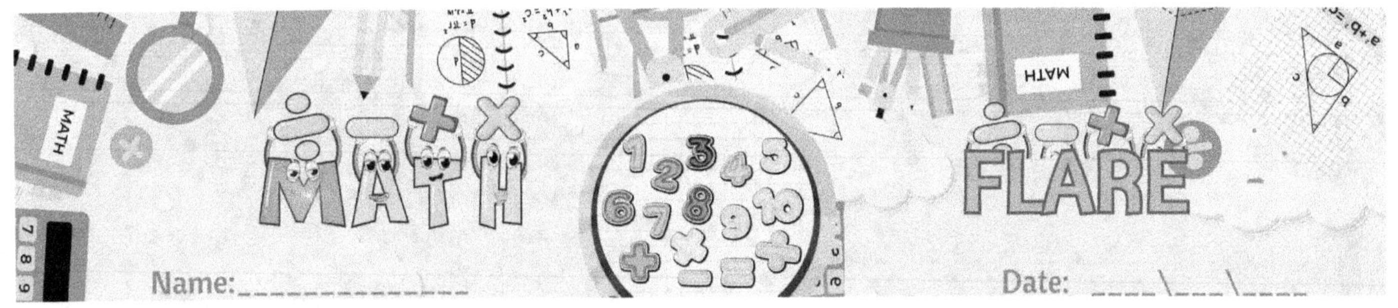

Addition Word Problems

1) Alice walked 8 miles yesterday and 16 miles today. How many miles did Alice walk in total?

$$\begin{array}{r} 8 \\ +\ 16 \\ \hline 24 \end{array}$$

    8   Alice rode 8 miles yesterday
 + 16   She rode 16 miles today
 24   She rode 24 miles in total

2) Lila has 5 liters of water in a container. She pours in 20 more liters of water. How much water is in the container now?

3) Olivia bought 2 towels and later bought 8 towels. How many towels does Olivia have now?

4) Gabriel has 11 pencils and 19 pens. If Gabriel puts all the writing utensils in a case, how many writing utensils are in the case in total?

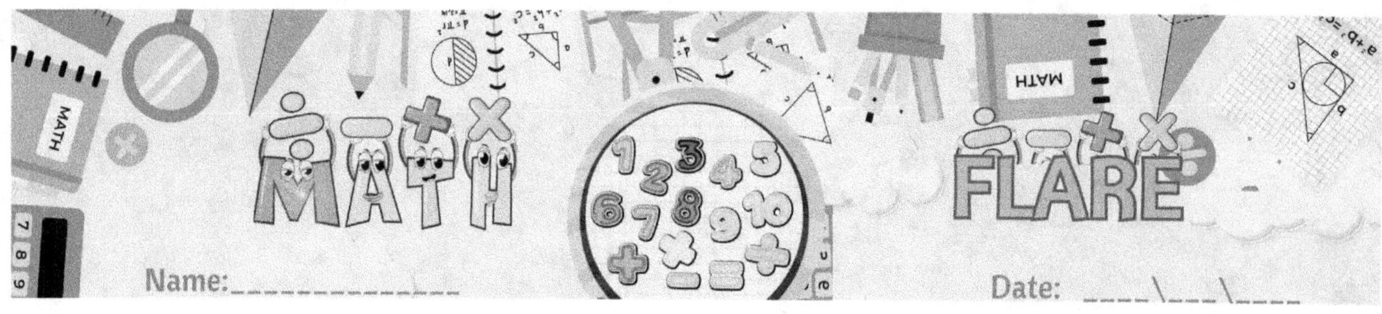

5) There are 11 crows on a tree. 11 more crows land on the tree. How many crows are on the tree now?

6) Caleb has 20 fish in an aquarium. If Caleb adds 12 more fish to the aquarium, how many fish will be in the aquarium in total?

7) Genesis sold 1 shoe on Monday and 18 shoes on Tuesday. How many shoes did the she sell in total?

8) Nova has 4 violins. Her friend gives her 11 more violins. How many violins does Nova have now?

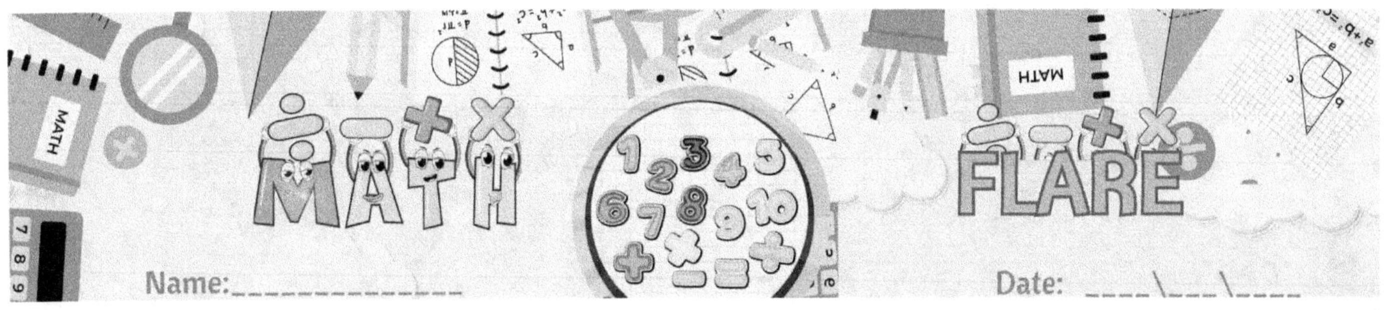

9) Jackson has 20 apples and 15 oranges in a basket. How many fruits does Jackson have in total?

10) There are 8 parrots on a tree. 15 more parrots land on the tree. How many parrots are on the tree now?

11) Kai had 1 dollars and earned 17 more dollars. How much money does Kai have now?

12) An object has 7 parts. If 5 more parts are added, how many parts does the object have now?

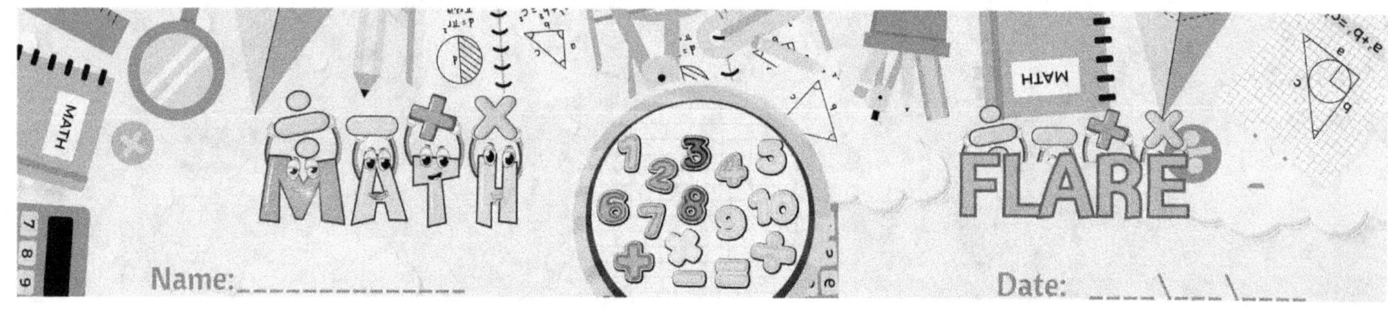

13) Nathaniel filled a tank with 2 gallons of gas and then added 19 more gallons. How many gallons of gas are in the tank now?

14) Aiden has 15 soaps. His sister gives him 8 more soaps . How many soaps does Aiden have now?

15) Sebastian has 14 toothpastes. He finds 13 more toothpastes. How many toothpastes does he have now?

16) There are 7 trees in the room. 20 more trees are brought in. How many trees are in the room now?

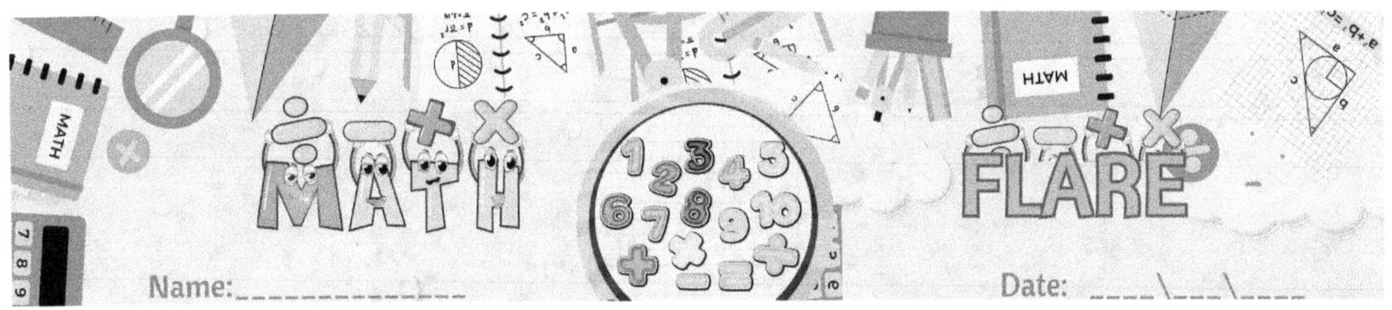

17) Levi has 12 surgical masks. He gets 8 more surgical masks. How many surgical masks does he have now?

18) There are 8 cats in the ground. 18 more cats come to play. How many cats are in the ground now?

19) Jordan has 12 cameras. He finds 2 more cameras on the ground. How many cameras does Jordan have now?

20) Benjamin has 16 gloves and buys 7 more gloves. How many gloves does Benjamin have in total?

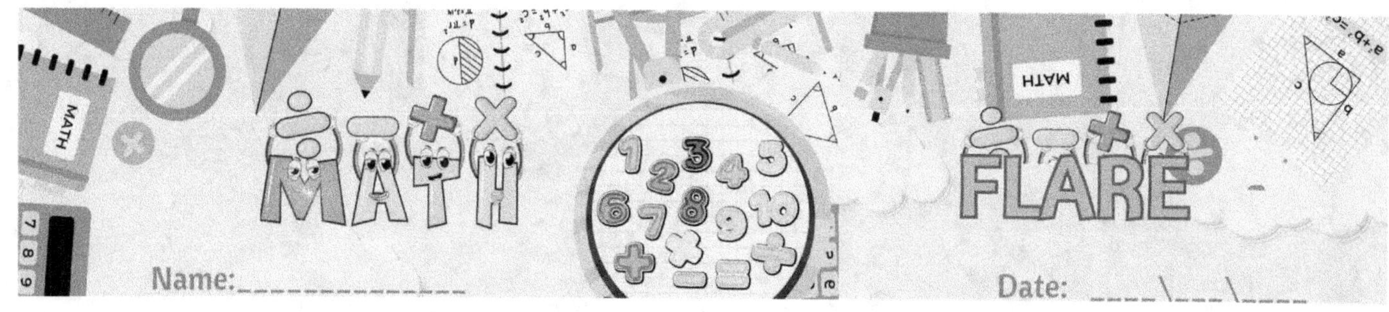

21) Aurora has 11 globes in a bag. If Aurora adds 20 more globes to the bag, how many globes does Aurora have in total?

22) Leo drove 16 miles in the morning and 15 miles in the evening. How many miles did Leo drive in total?

23) Aaron has 16 perfumes and 8 more perfumes are added to the collection. How many perfumes does Aaron have in total?

24) There are 15 fishes in the pond. 14 more fishes join them. How many fishes are in the pond now?

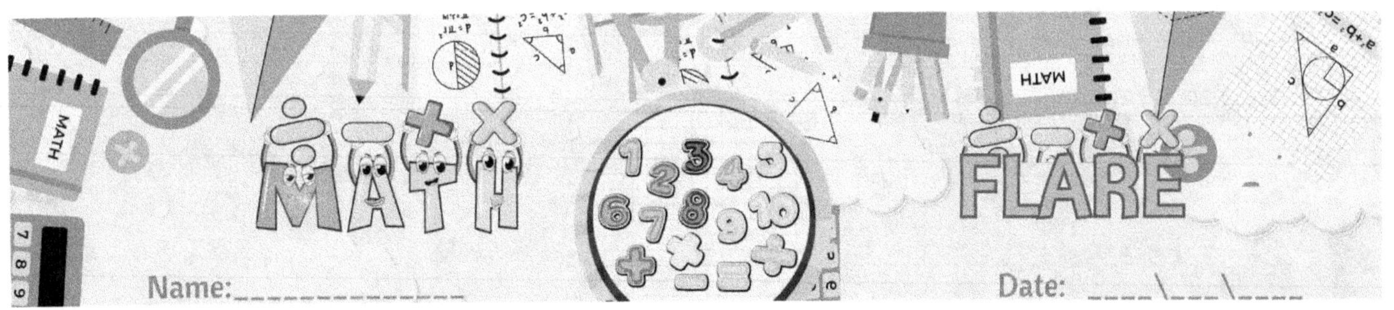

25) Jaxon has 18 pianos. He gets 3 more pianos as a gift. How many pianos does Jaxon have now?

26) At the store, Oliver bought 19 scarves. Later, Madeline bought 15 scarves from the same store. How many scarves were bought in total?

27) There are 16 kids playing on the playground. 3 more kids join them. How many kids are playing now?

28) Jason made 1 cookies and Leah made 11 cookies. How many cookies were made in total?

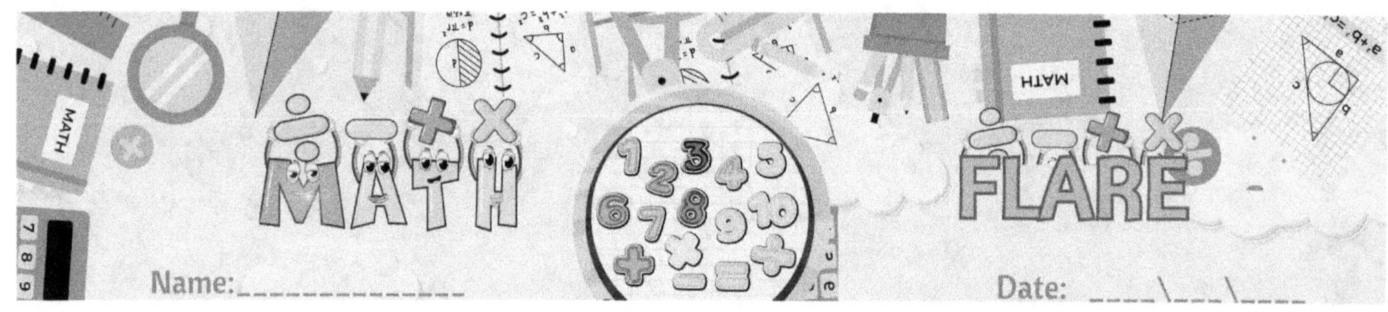

29) Luna has 9 bananas. She buys 1 more banana at the store. How many bananas does Luna have now?

30) Ethan has 18 red marbles and 3 blue marbles in a jar. How many marbles does Ethan have in total?

31) There are 13 gauzes on the shelf. Alexa puts 4 more gauzes on the shelf. How many gauzes are there on the shelf now?

32) Lucas has 5 spoons. He receives 19 more spoons. How many spoons does he have now?

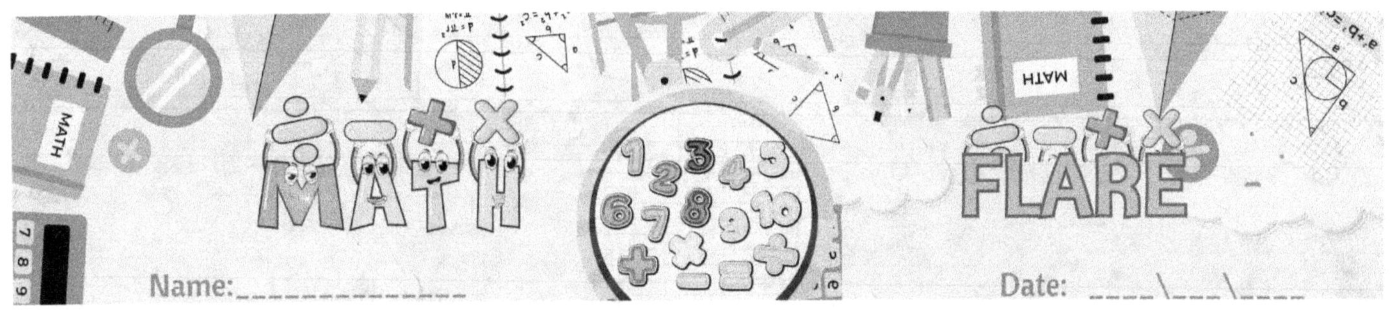

33) Dylan has 5 bagels. He finds 1 more bagel. How many bagels does he have now?

34) Miles bought a bag of scalpels for 1 dollars. Later, Miles bought another bag of scalpels for 13 dollars. How much money did Miles spend in total?

35) Elena has 11 flowers. She buys 6 more flowers at the store. How many flowers does Elena have now?

36) There are 20 trees in the garden. 18 more trees are planted. How many trees are in the garden now?

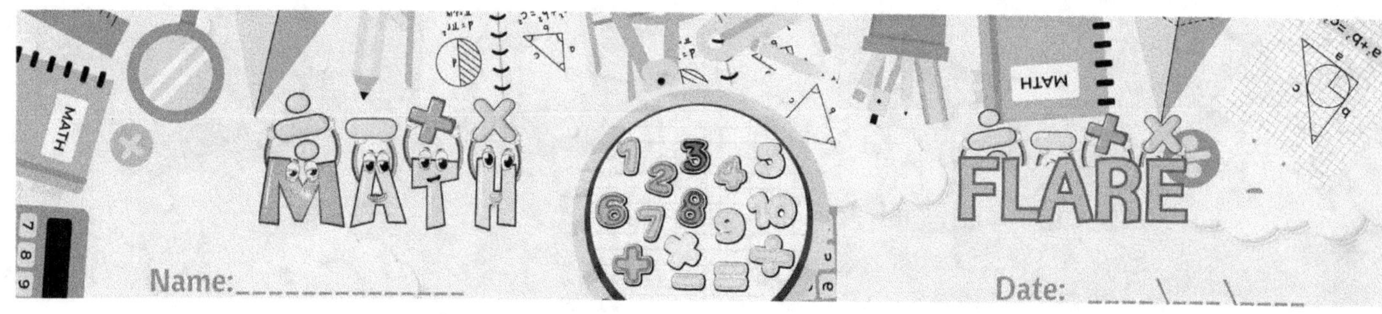

37) Brody baked 20 cookies and 1 cupcakes. How many desserts did Brody bake in total?

38) There are 4 cakes in the bag. If 1 more cake is added, how many cakes are in the bag now?

39) On Monday, Hazel caught 2 fish, and on Tuesday, Hazel caught 13 fish. How many fish did Hazel catch in total?

40) Liam has 10 mirrors. He buys 14 more mirrors. How many mirrors does she have now?

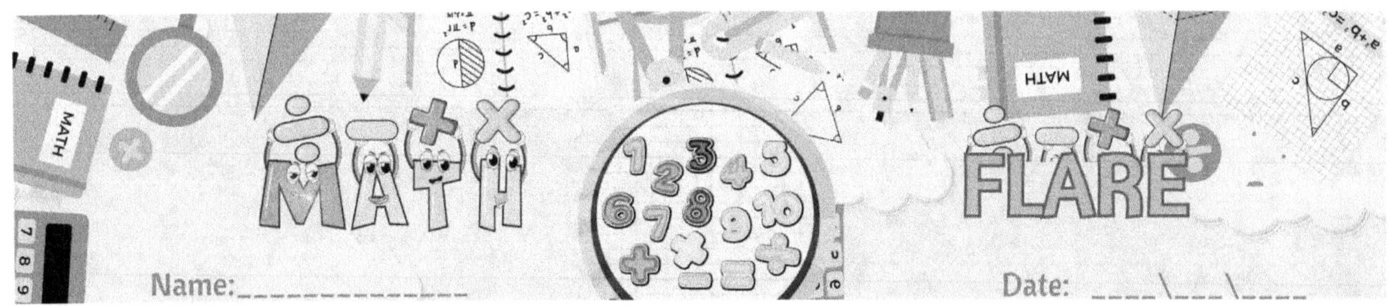

Subtraction Word Problems

1) There are 2 calculators in a bag. Samantha took 2 calculators out of the bag. How many calculators are still in the bag?

$$
\begin{array}{r}
2 \\
-\ 2 \\
\hline
0
\end{array}
$$

there are 2 calculators in the bag
Samantha took 2 calculators
there are 0 calculators in the bag

2) Amy bought toothbrushes for 6 dollars. She received 4 dollars in change. How much did toothbrushes cost?

3) A cake recipe calls for 2 cups of flour. 1 cups of flour have already been added. How many more cups of flour are needed?

4) A cake recipe requires 9 cups of sugar. Sharon only has 5 cups of sugar. How many more cups of sugar does Sharon need?

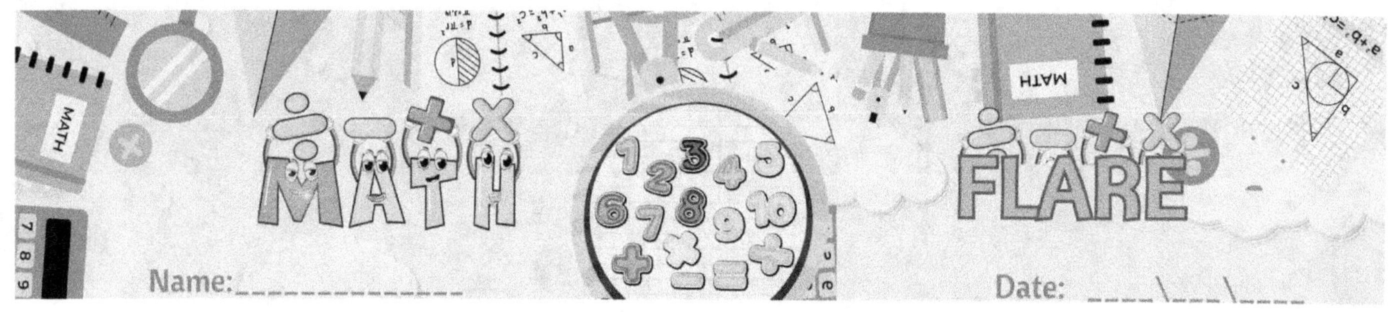

5) A small bag of chips has 2 chips in it. John ate 2 chips. How many chips are left in the bag?

6) Sharon has 4 compasses. She lost 4 of them. How many compasses does Sharon have left?

7) Jackie has 3 dollars. She wants to buy pencils, which costs 6 dollars. How much more money does she need to buy it?

8) Marin had 2 dollars. She spent 2 dollars on dresses. How much money does Marin have left?

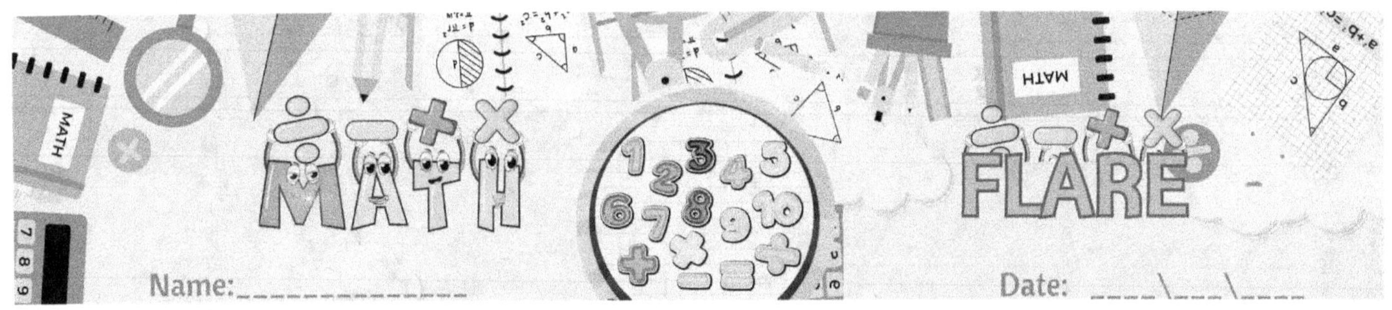

9) Robert has 2 red breads and 2 green breads. How many more red breads does Robert have than green breads?

10) Scarves originally cost 8 dollars, but it is now on sale for 8 dollars. How much money can you save by buying it on sale?

11) Stephanie and Betty went shopping for pens. They had 5 dollars to spend but 3 dollars ended up being spent. How much money do they have left?

12) Jessica wants to buy coins, which costs 2 dollars. She has 2 dollars and plans to save the rest. How much more money does she need to save to buy coins?

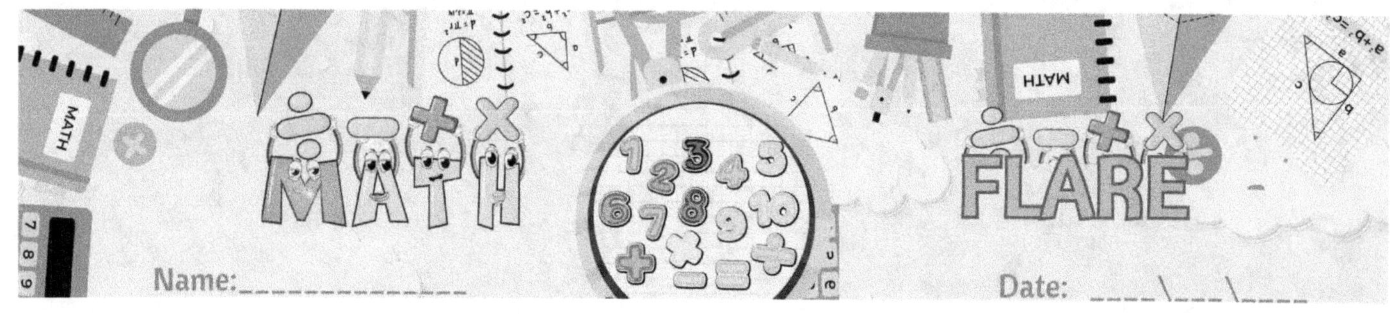

13) Richard had 7 forks. He gave 2 forks to Marcie. How many forks does Richard have left?

14) Deborah bought gloves for 7 dollars but later found out it was on sale for 4 dollars less. How much did she overpay for gloves?

15) A box had 3 chocolates. Michele ate 3 chocolates. How many chocolates are left in the box?

16) A box of pants weighs 5 pounds. If you remove 2 pounds from it, how much does it weigh now?

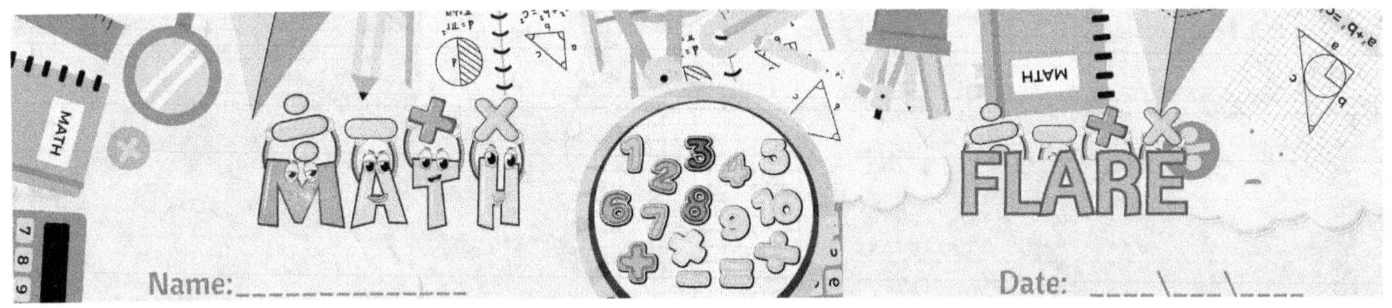

17) Robert has 2 dollars. He needs to buy ointments that costs 4 dollars. How much money will he have left after buying the ointments?

18) A pack of gum had 3 pieces. Stephanie took 3 pieces of gum. How many pieces of gum are left in the pack?

19) If spoons costs 4 dollars and you have 4 dollars, how much more money do you need to buy it?

20) Richard had 10 dollars. He spent 7 dollars on a hats. How much money does Richard have left?

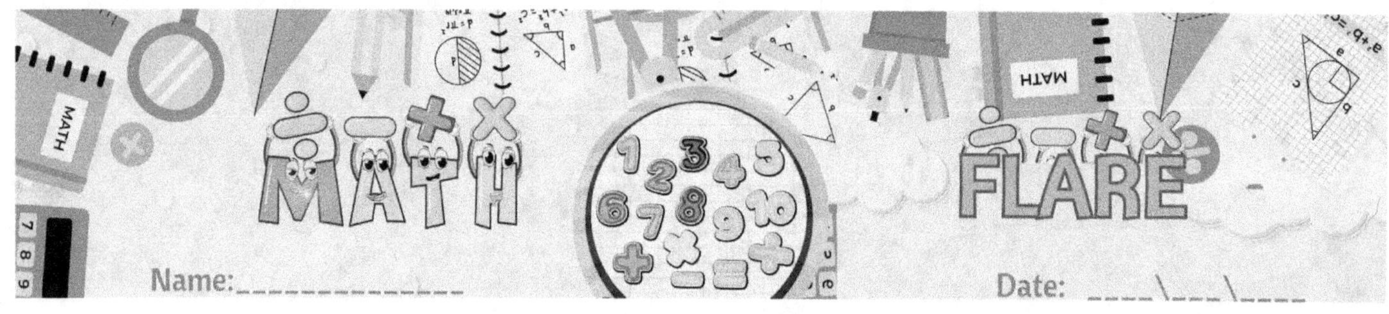

21) Stethoscopes costs 9 dollars. If you paid $6. How much change will you get back?

22) A recipe needs 5 cups of sugar. Marin added 3 cups of sugar. How many cups of sugar are still needed?

23) Adam is 10 years old and Paul is 7 years old. What is the difference in their ages?

24) There were 2 students in a class. 1 of them were absent. How many students were present in the class?

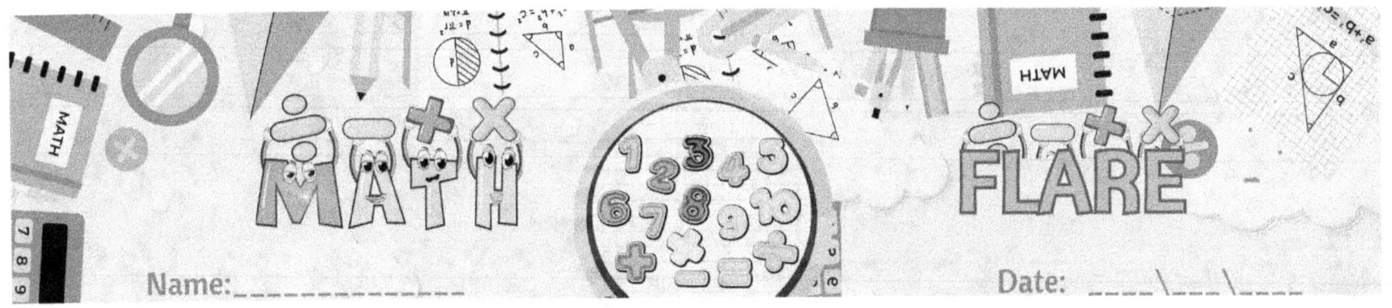

25) James has 7 plates in his collection. He sold 7 of them at a sale. How many plates does he have left in his collection?

26) Elizabeth has 9 shampoos. She gave 4 shampoos to Janet. How many shampoos does Elizabeth have now?

27) Samantha baked a 7 cookies. 3 of them were chocolate chip cookies and the rest were oatmeal raisin cookies. How many oatmeal raisin cookies did Samantha bake?

28) Donald has 5 toothpastes. He traded 1 of them with his friend. How many toothpastes does Donald have now?

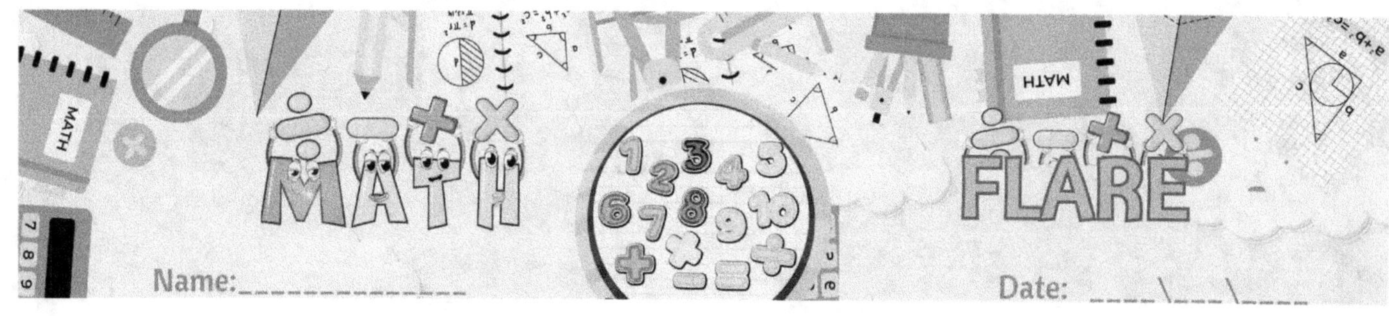

29) A cameras costs $8 and a pen costs $6. How much more expensive is the cameras than the pen?

30) There are 9 fish in a tank. If 8 leave, how many fish are left in the tank?

31) There are 7 cars in a parking lot. Anthony took 2 cars out of the lot. How many cars are still in the lot?

32) Daniel saved up 6 dollars to buy computers. He spent 3 dollars on it. How much money does he have left?

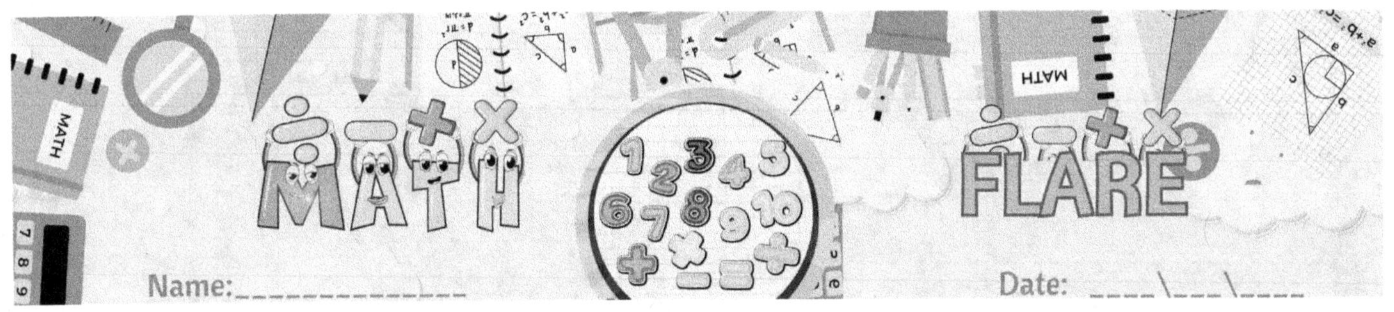

33) If you have 10 needles and you give away 4, how many needles do you have left?

34) There are 3 dogs in a park. If 3 leave, how many dogs are left in the park?

35) Amanda and Debra went on a shopping spree and bought 7 calendars. After returning home, they realized that they didn't need 2 of them. How many calendars did they end up keeping?

36) There are 2 fish in a pond. Jackie caught 1 fish. How many fish are left in the pond?

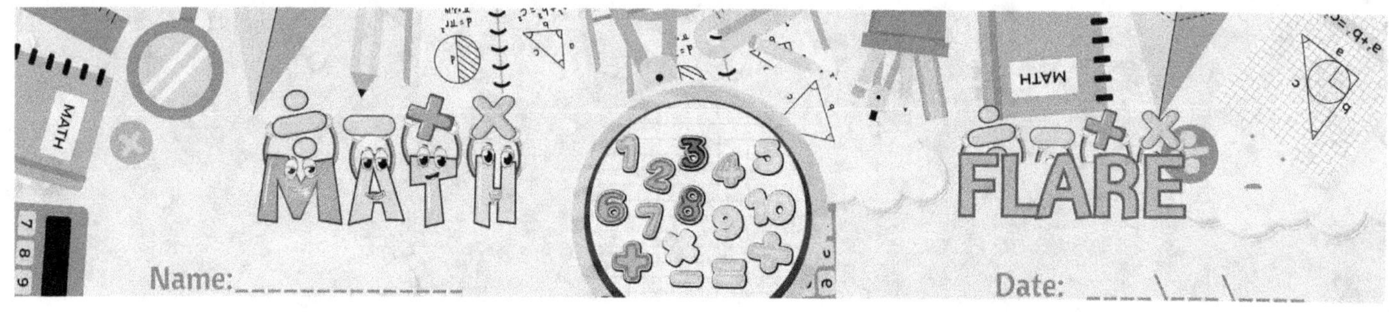

37) There are 9 turtles in a pond. If 3 leave, how many turtles are left in the pond?

38) There are 5 thermometers. 4 thermometers are blue and the rest are red. How many red thermometers are in the box?

39) Christopher has 4 dollars. He wants to buy balls that costs 4 dollars. How much more money does he need to buy the balls?

40) Sharon bought notebooks for 6 dollars. She later returned some notebooks and received a refund of 1 dollars. How much money did she end up spending on notebooks?

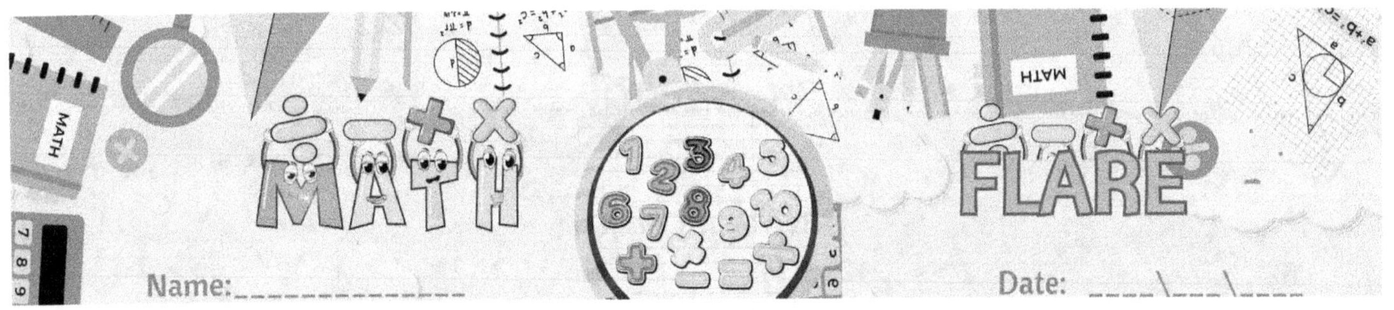

41) Ashley has 9 lotions in her collection. She gave 2 of them to her friend. How many lotions does Ashley have now?

42) Barbara and Jennifer had 9 shirts altogether. Jennifer gave 9 shirts to Paul. How many shirts do they have left?

43) A pizza has 9 slices. Ellen ate 2 slices. How many slices of pizza are left?

44) Nicholas has 5 apples. He traded 5 of them with his friend. How many apples does Nicholas have now?

Chapter. 02

Multiplication

Multiplication

Multiplication is an easy way of adding numbers together quickly. Instead of adding the same number repeatedly, we use multiplication to find the total much faster.

For instance, rather than adding 2 + 2 + 2 + 2 + 2, we can multiply 2 by 5 to get the same result: 2 x 5 = 10.

Here, the first number (2) is called the multiplicand, second number (5) is the multiplier. The answer we get, in this case, 10, is called the product.

Let's think of multiplication as repeated addition.

Take 2 x 5, for example. It means adding 2 together five times, which we can illustrate as: 2 + 2 + 2 + 2 + 2 = 10

Multiplication can also be visualized as groups of objects. Imagine we have 2 groups, each containing 5 oranges.

To find the total number of oranges, we multiply the number of groups (2) by the number of oranges in each group (5):

2 groups of 5 oranges = 10 oranges

Expressed as multiplication: 2 x 5 = 10

In summary, multiplication offers various ways to approach it: through repeated addition or by envisioning groups of objects. It's a powerful tool that makes solving math problems much quicker and more efficient!

We can also use the following table to quickly remember multiplication facts. The intersection of two points shows the product of two numbers.

For instance, the product of 5 x 6 = 30, or 6 x 5 = 30.

	1	2	3	4	5	6	7	8	9	10
1	1	2	3	4	5	6	7	8	9	10
2	2	4	6	8	10	12	14	16	18	20
3	3	6	9	12	15	18	21	24	27	30
4	4	8	12	16	20	24	28	32	36	40
5	5	10	15	20	25	30	35	40	45	50
6	6	12	18	24	30	36	42	48	54	60
7	7	14	21	28	35	42	49	56	63	70
8	8	16	24	32	40	48	56	64	72	80
9	9	18	27	36	45	54	63	72	81	90
10	10	20	30	40	50	60	70	80	90	100

Let's solve problems from exercises:

$$
\begin{array}{rr}
20 & 10 \\
\times\ \ 4 & \times\ \ 7 \\
\hline
80 & 70
\end{array}
$$

MathFlare - Math Workbook 2nd and 3rd Grade

Commutative Property of Multiplication

The commutative property of multiplication is a special rule in math that tells us the order of the numbers being multiplied doesn't affect the result.

For instance, let's take 2 x 5. If we switch the order of the numbers, multiplying 5 by 2 instead, we'll still end up with the same answer: 2 x 5 = 10, or 5 x 2 = 10.

So, whether we multiply 2 by 5 or 5 by 2, we get 10. That's the commutative property of multiplication in action!

Division

Division is like the opposite of multiplication. It's all about sharing or distributing items equally among a certain number of groups or people.

When we divide one number by another, we're essentially splitting a number into equal parts. We're figuring out how many groups of a certain size can be made from that number.

For instance, let's divide 20 by 4.

When we divide 20 by 4, we're essentially asking, "How many groups of size 4 can we make from 20?"

Now, there are several parts or terms involved in the division process:

- Dividend: This is the number being divided, which in this case, is 20.

- Divisor: This is the number we're dividing by, which is 4.

- Quotient: This is the answer we get after dividing. It tells us how many groups of the divisor can be made from the dividend. In this case, the answer is 5.

So, when we divide 20 by 4, we found out that 5 groups of 4 can be made from 20.

Let's solve problems from exercises:

$$
\begin{array}{r}
18 \\
2\overline{)36} \\
-2 \\
\hline
16 \\
-16 \\
\hline
0
\end{array}
\qquad
\begin{array}{r}
5 \\
2\overline{)10} \\
-10 \\
\hline
0
\end{array}
$$

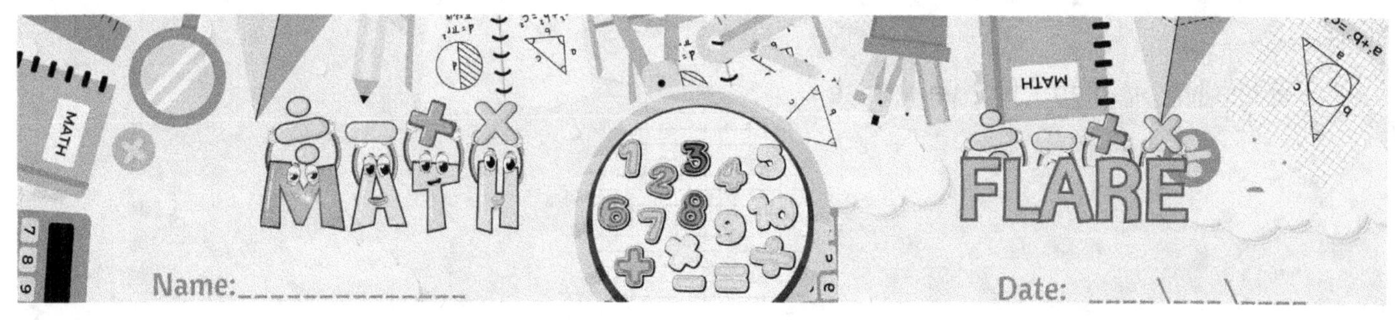

Multiplication by 1

1) 1
× 5
    5

2) 1
× 1
    1

3) 1
× 6

4) 3
× 1

5) 8
× 1

6) 1
× 4

7) 2
× 1

8) 9
× 1

9) 7
× 1

10) 1
× 3

11) 1
× 8

12) 6
× 1

13) 1
× 7

14) 1
× 9

15) 4
× 1

16) 5
× 1

17) 1
× 2

18) 1
× 8

19) 4
× 1

20) 5
× 1

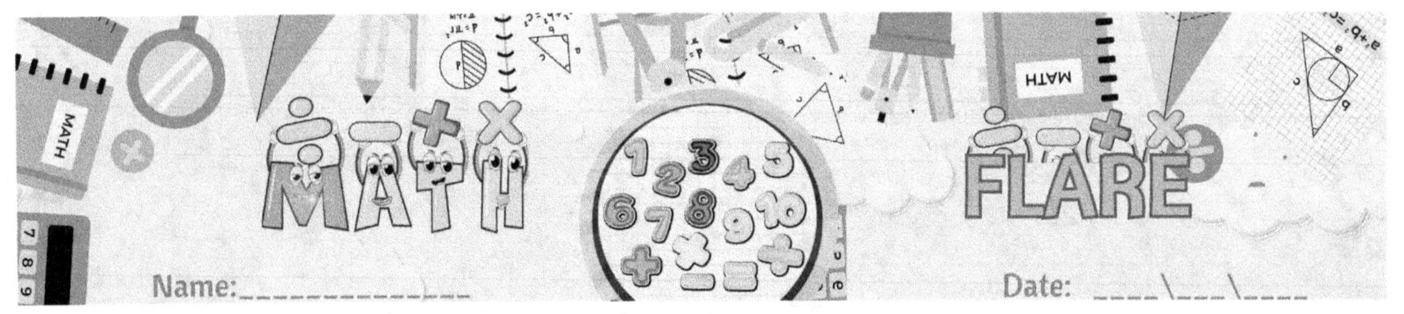

Multiplication by 2

1) 2
  × 2

2) 5
  × 2

3) 4
  × 2

4) 2
  × 3

5) 2
  × 6

6) 2
  × 9

7) 1
  × 2

8) 8
  × 2

9) 2
  × 7

10) 2
  × 8

11) 2
  × 5

12) 3
  × 2

13) 7
  × 2

14) 2
  × 4

15) 2
  × 1

16) 9
  × 2

17) 6
  × 2

18) 4
  × 2

19) 2
  × 1

20) 3
  × 2

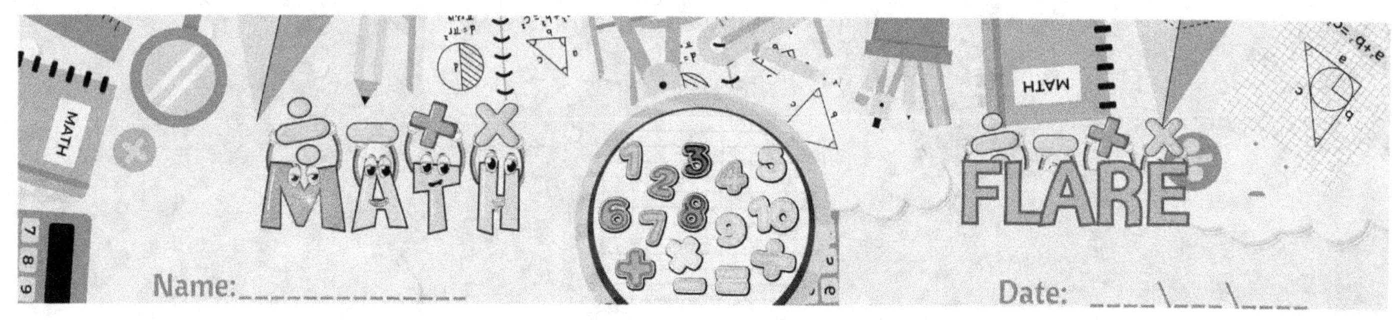

Multiplication by 3

1) 3
 × 6
────

2) 3
 × 3
────

3) 3
 × 8
────

4) 9
 × 3
────

5) 3
 × 7
────

6) 2
 × 3
────

7) 4
 × 3
────

8) 5
 × 3
────

9) 1
 × 3
────

10) 3
 × 2
────

11) 3
 × 4
────

12) 3
 × 5
────

13) 8
 × 3
────

14) 7
 × 3
────

15) 6
 × 3
────

16) 3
 × 9
────

17) 3
 × 1
────

18) 3
 × 3
────

19) 3
 × 6
────

20) 6
 × 3
────

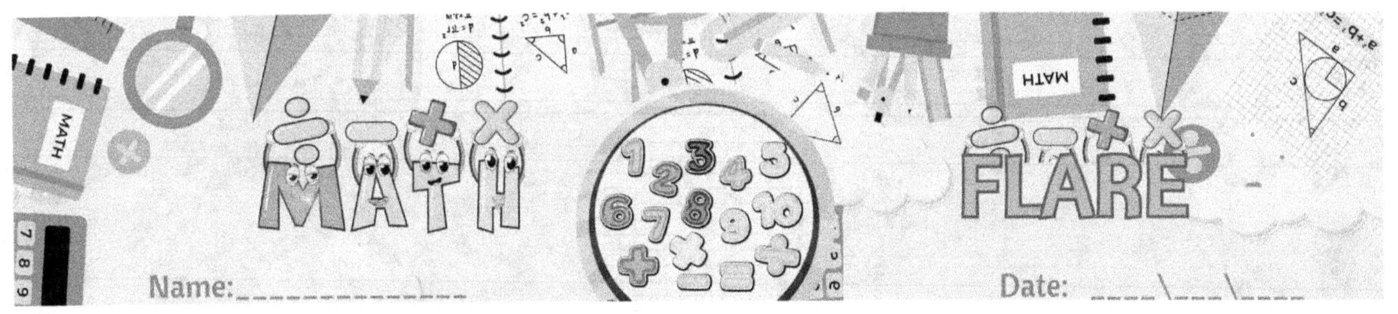

Multiplication by 4

1) 6
   × 4

2) 4
   × 3

3) 5
   × 4

4) 7
   × 4

5) 2
   × 4

6) 1
   × 4

7) 4
   × 4

8) 9
   × 4

9) 8
   × 4

10) 4
    × 2

11) 4
    × 5

12) 4
    × 8

13) 4
    × 6

14) 3
    × 4

15) 4
    × 7

16) 4
    × 1

17) 4
    × 9

18) 6
    × 4

19) 4
    × 5

20) 4
    × 6

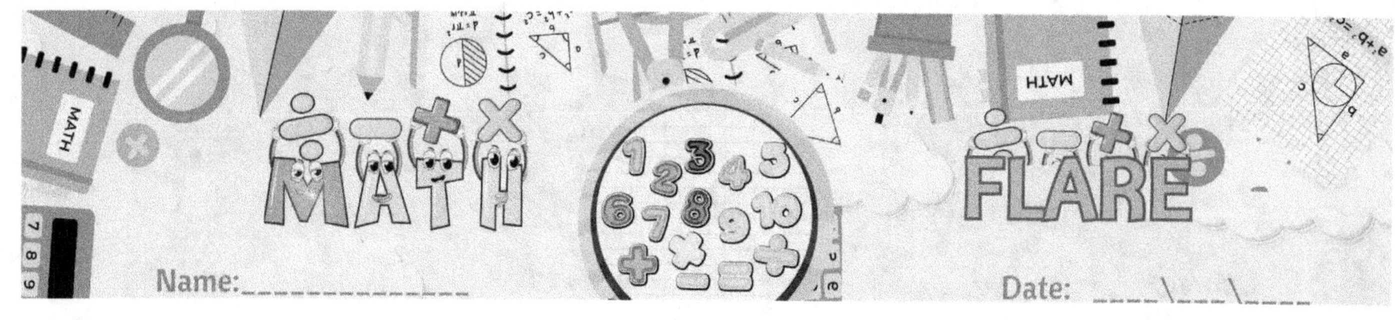

Multiplication by 5

1) 5
   × 4

2) 5
   × 3

3) 5
   × 2

4) 5
   × 5

5) 5
   × 1

6) 6
   × 5

7) 5
   × 7

8) 5
   × 8

9) 5
   × 9

10) 7
    × 5

11) 4
    × 5

12) 5
    × 6

13) 3
    × 5

14) 8
    × 5

15) 9
    × 5

16) 1
    × 5

17) 2
    × 5

18) 3
    × 5

19) 5
    × 8

20) 2
    × 5

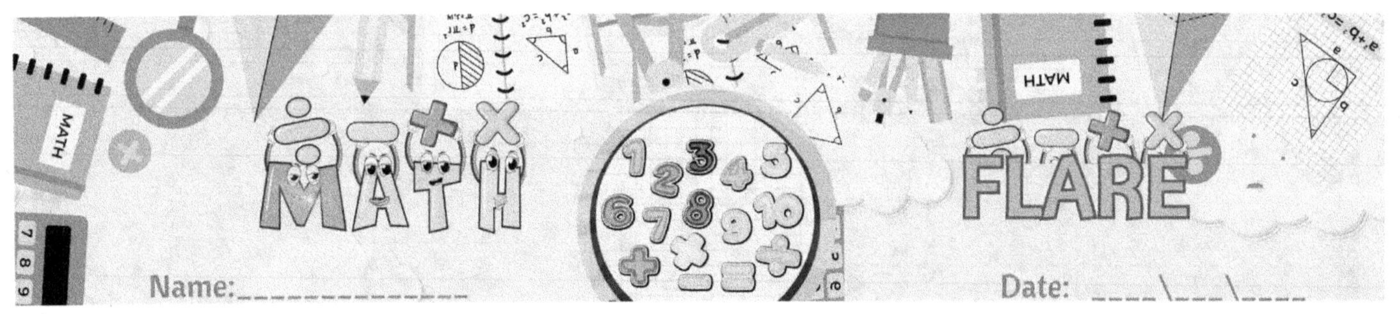

Multiplication by 6

1)   2
 × 6
  12

2)   6
 × 8
  48

3)   9
 × 6

4)   6
 × 7

5)   6
 × 1

6)   5
 × 6

7)   6
 × 6

8)   3
 × 6

9)   6
 × 4

10)   7
 × 6

11)   4
 × 6

12)   8
 × 6

13)   6
 × 3

14)   6
 × 5

15)   1
 × 6

16)   6
 × 2

17)   6
 × 9

18)   6
 × 4

19)   6
 × 6

20)   6
 × 5

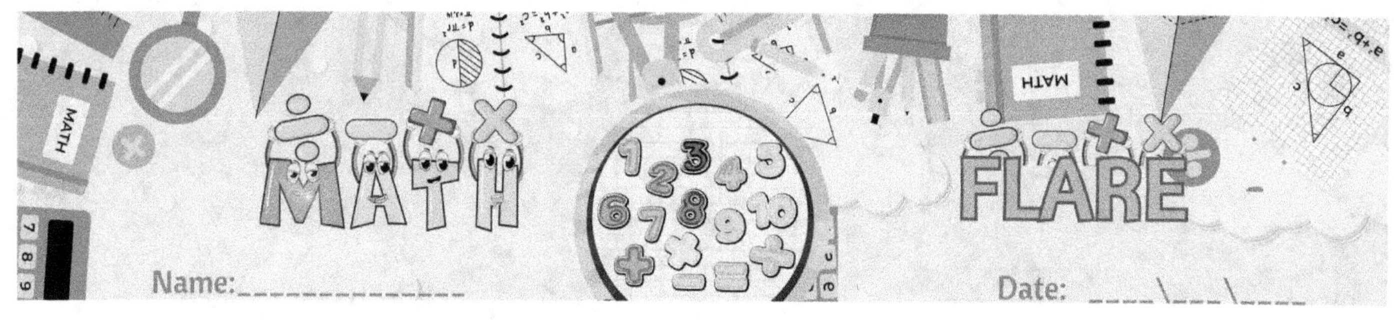

Multiplication by 7

1)　　7
　　× 5

2)　　7
　　× 7

3)　　1
　　× 7

4)　　7
　　× 4

5)　　6
　　× 7

6)　　7
　　× 2

7)　　8
　　× 7

8)　　7
　　× 3

9)　　7
　　× 9

10)　　2
　　× 7

11)　　4
　　× 7

12)　　5
　　× 7

13)　　7
　　× 8

14)　　7
　　× 1

15)　　9
　　× 7

16)　　3
　　× 7

17)　　7
　　× 6

18)　　4
　　× 7

19)　　7
　　× 7

20)　　7
　　× 7

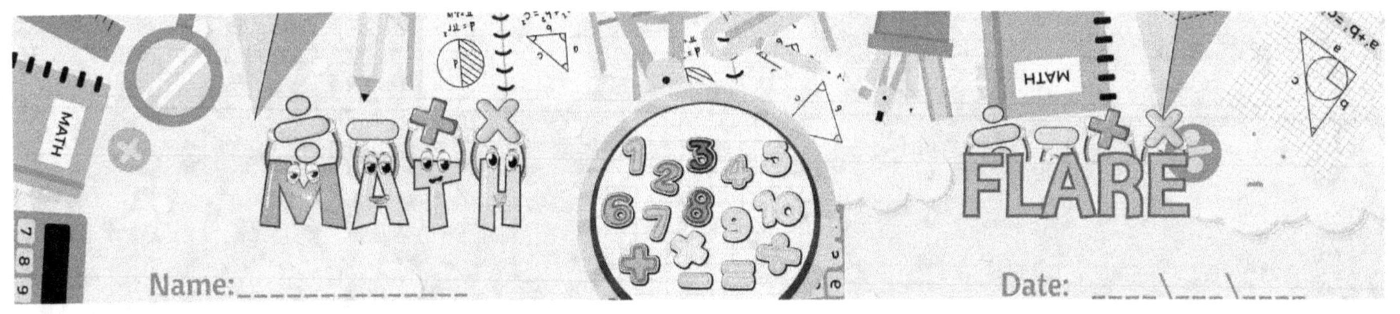

Multiplication by 8

1) 8
× 1

2) 8
× 8

3) 8
× 6

4) 8
× 2

5) 7
× 8

6) 8
× 9

7) 8
× 4

8) 8
× 5

9) 8
× 3

10) 1
× 8

11) 4
× 8

12) 5
× 8

13) 8
× 7

14) 2
× 8

15) 9
× 8

16) 6
× 8

17) 3
× 8

18) 8
× 5

19) 9
× 8

20) 5
× 8

Multiplication by 9

1)   9
  × 7

2)   8
  × 9

3)   6
  × 9

4)   2
  × 9

5)   9
  × 5

6)   1
  × 9

7)   9
  × 9

8)   9
  × 3

9)   4
  × 9

10)   9
  × 2

11)   9
  × 4

12)   5
  × 9

13)   3
  × 9

14)   9
  × 8

15)   9
  × 6

16)   7
  × 9

17)   9
  × 1

18)   3
  × 9

19)   5
  × 9

20)   9
  × 7

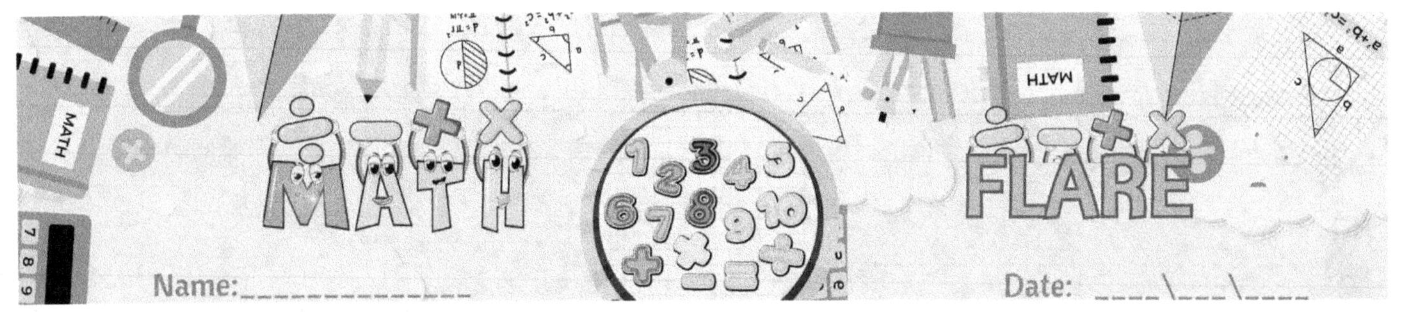

Multiplication by 10

1)　　10
　　× 7

2)　　 3
　　× 10

3)　　10
　　× 2

4)　　 8
　　× 10

5)　　10
　　× 9

6)　　 6
　　× 10

7)　　 5
　　× 10

8)　　 1
　　× 10

9)　　10
　　× 4

10)　　 7
　　× 10

11)　　10
　　× 5

12)　　10
　　× 1

13)　　10
　　× 3

14)　　10
　　× 6

15)　　 2
　　× 10

16)　　10
　　× 8

17)　　 4
　　× 10

18)　　 9
　　× 10

19)　　10
　　× 3

20)　　 6
　　× 10

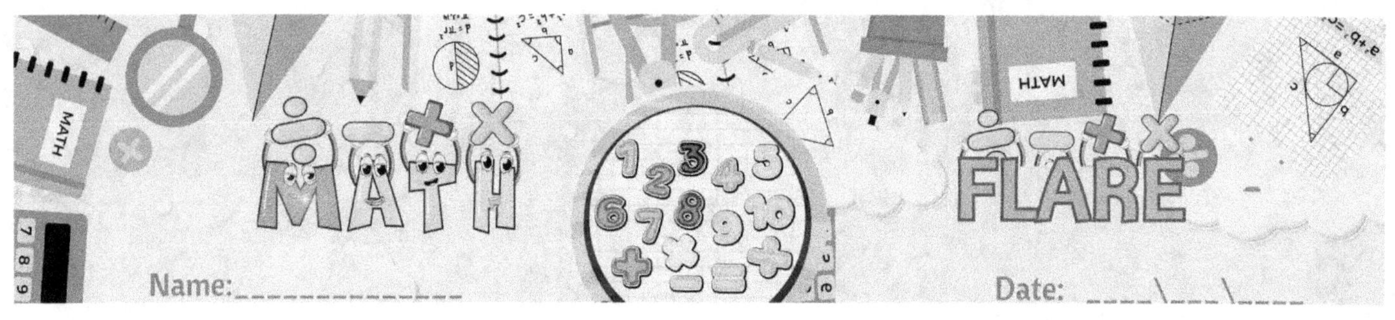

Multiplication
Find the product.

1) 7
  × 8
  56

2) 7
  × 3
  21

3) 3
  × 4

4) 1
  × 10

5) 3
  × 3

6) 10
  × 5

7) 3
  × 6

8) 4
  × 4

9) 4
  × 7

10) 8
  × 3

11) 9
  × 9

12) 4
  × 9

13) 5
  × 7

14) 6
  × 2

15) 2
  × 7

16) 6
  × 6

17) 6
  × 1

18) 10
  × 4

19) 5
  × 9

20) 9
  × 7

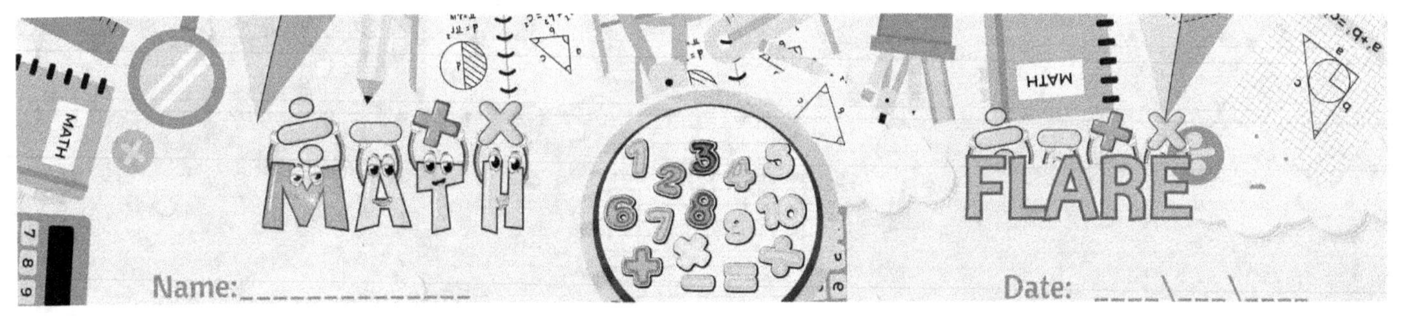

21) 5
   × 2

22) 5
   × 5

23) 9
   × 4

24) 1
   × 7

25) 6
   × 4

26) 8
   × 8

27) 5
   × 8

28) 9
   × 6

29) 8
   × 10

30) 6
   × 8

31) 10
   × 3

32) 4
   × 1

33) 2
   × 9

34) 5
   × 3

35) 6
   × 3

36) 6
   × 10

37) 2
   × 8

38) 9
   × 8

39) 6
   × 7

40) 3
   × 7

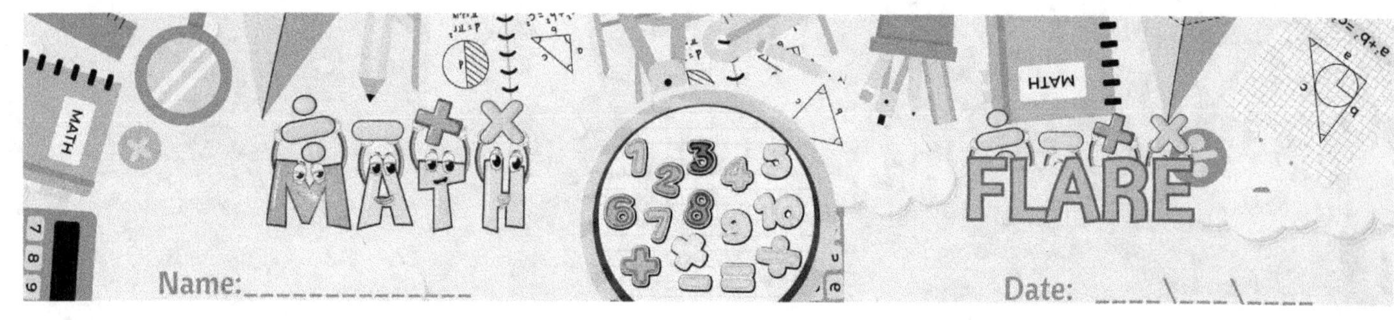

41) 10
   × 1

42) 10
   × 6

43)   3
   × 9

44)   6
   × 5

45)   8
   × 1

46)   1
   × 6

47)   9
   × 3

48)   7
   × 2

49)   7
   × 6

50)   4
   × 8

51)   7
   × 9

52)   4
   × 10

53)   2
   × 5

54)   2
   × 6

55)   8
   × 2

56)   6
   × 9

57)   2
   × 2

58) 10
   × 9

59)   9
   × 5

60)   9
   × 1

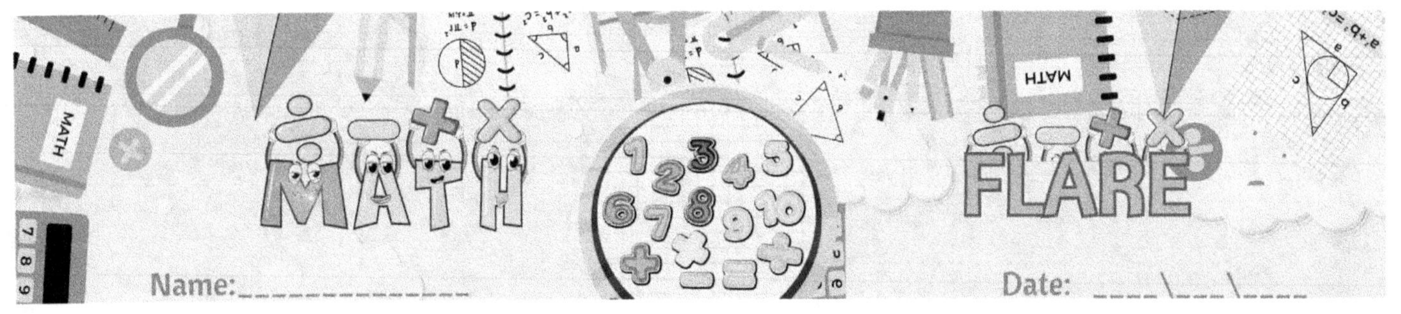

61)   1
× 1

62)   5
× 6

63)   4
× 5

64)   9
× 10

65)   5
× 4

66)   10
× 8

67)   8
× 4

68)   1
× 4

69)   9
× 2

70)   8
× 7

71)   2
× 3

72)   7
× 10

73)   4
× 6

74)   5
× 1

75)   8
× 5

76)   1
× 8

77)   2
× 4

78)   10
× 2

79)   3
× 5

80)   10
× 7

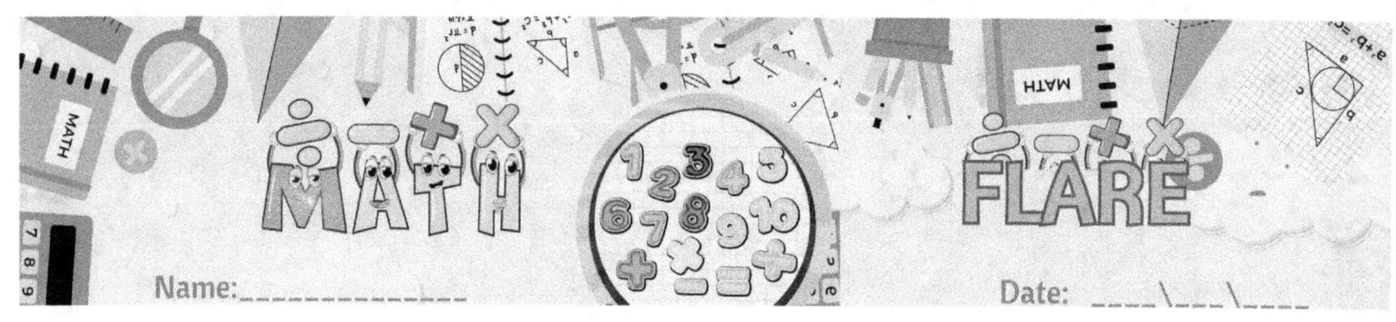

81) $\begin{array}{r} 3 \\ \times\ 10 \\ \hline \end{array}$	82) $\begin{array}{r} 4 \\ \times\ 3 \\ \hline \end{array}$	83) $\begin{array}{r} 3 \\ \times\ 2 \\ \hline \end{array}$	84) $\begin{array}{r} 8 \\ \times\ 9 \\ \hline \end{array}$
85) $\begin{array}{r} 3 \\ \times\ 8 \\ \hline \end{array}$	86) $\begin{array}{r} 7 \\ \times\ 5 \\ \hline \end{array}$	87) $\begin{array}{r} 7 \\ \times\ 7 \\ \hline \end{array}$	88) $\begin{array}{r} 4 \\ \times\ 2 \\ \hline \end{array}$
89) $\begin{array}{r} 8 \\ \times\ 6 \\ \hline \end{array}$	90) $\begin{array}{r} 2 \\ \times\ 1 \\ \hline \end{array}$	91) $\begin{array}{r} 1 \\ \times\ 9 \\ \hline \end{array}$	92) $\begin{array}{r} 7 \\ \times\ 4 \\ \hline \end{array}$
93) $\begin{array}{r} 2 \\ \times\ 10 \\ \hline \end{array}$	94) $\begin{array}{r} 5 \\ \times\ 10 \\ \hline \end{array}$	95) $\begin{array}{r} 7 \\ \times\ 1 \\ \hline \end{array}$	96) $\begin{array}{r} 10 \\ \times\ 10 \\ \hline \end{array}$
97) $\begin{array}{r} 3 \\ \times\ 1 \\ \hline \end{array}$	98) $\begin{array}{r} 1 \\ \times\ 3 \\ \hline \end{array}$	99) $\begin{array}{r} 1 \\ \times\ 2 \\ \hline \end{array}$	100) $\begin{array}{r} 1 \\ \times\ 5 \\ \hline \end{array}$

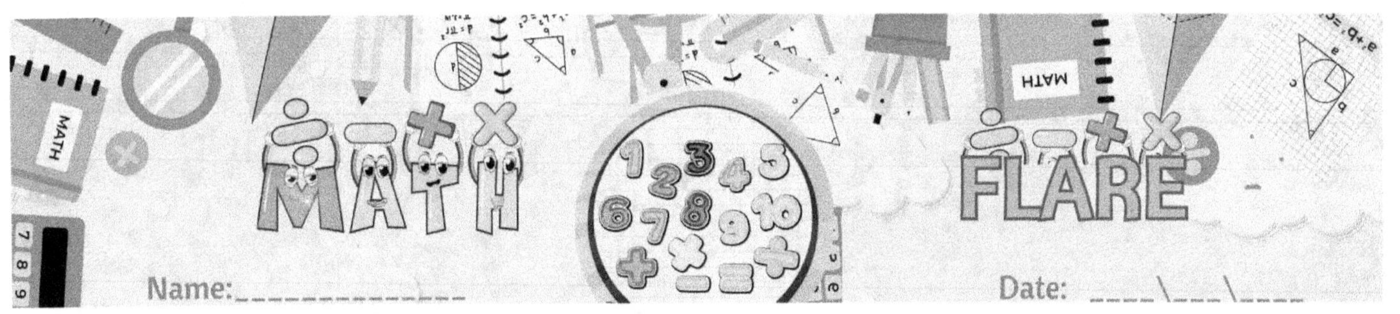

Multiplication: 2 x 1

Find the product.

1) 20
  × 4

2) 21
  × 4

3) 22
  × 4

4) 21
  × 3

5) 43
  × 2

6) 61
  × 1

7) 13
  × 3

8) 31
  × 2

9) 21
  × 2

10) 12
  × 4

11) 33
  × 3

12) 20
  × 3

13) 13
  × 2

14) 23
  × 2

15) 55
  × 1

16) 22
  × 3

17) 34
  × 2

18) 23
  × 3

19) 12
  × 1

20) 68
  × 1

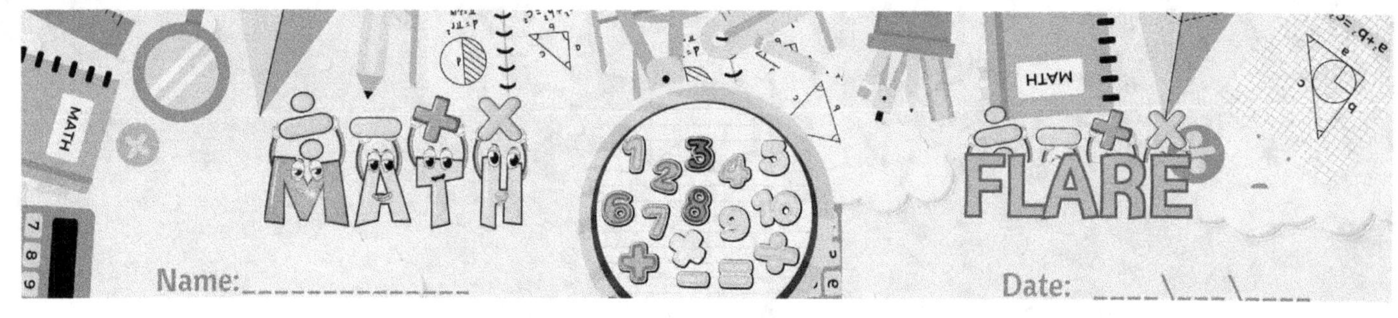

21) 11 × 3	22) 20 × 2	23) 31 × 3	24) 25 × 1
25) 10 × 4	26) 32 × 3	27) 30 × 3	28) 11 × 4
29) 10 × 5	30) 98 × 1	31) 12 × 3	32) 22 × 2
33) 24 × 2	34) 14 × 2	35) 40 × 2	36) 78 × 1
37) 11 × 5	38) 44 × 2	39) 86 × 1	40) 54 × 1

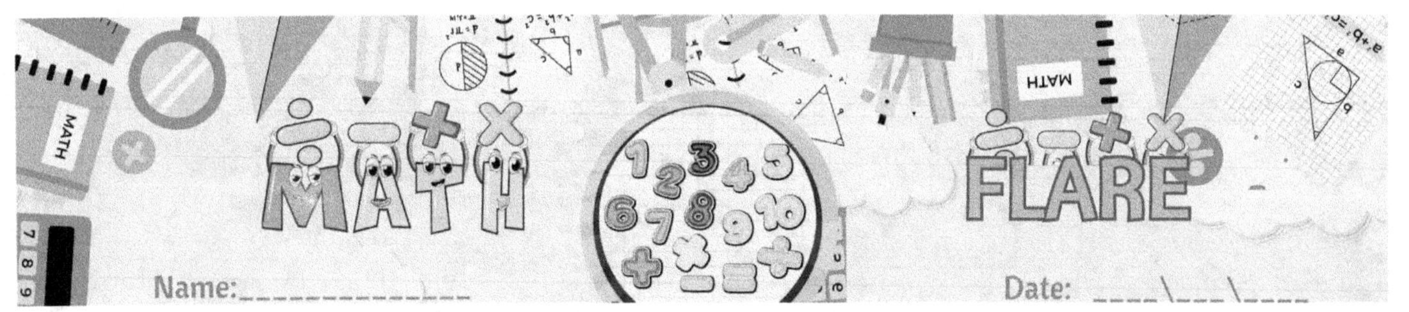

41) $\begin{array}{r} 30 \\ \times\ 2 \\ \hline \end{array}$	42) $\begin{array}{r} 10 \\ \times\ 3 \\ \hline \end{array}$	43) $\begin{array}{r} 42 \\ \times\ 2 \\ \hline \end{array}$	44) $\begin{array}{r} 41 \\ \times\ 2 \\ \hline \end{array}$
45) $\begin{array}{r} 33 \\ \times\ 2 \\ \hline \end{array}$	46) $\begin{array}{r} 52 \\ \times\ 1 \\ \hline \end{array}$	47) $\begin{array}{r} 11 \\ \times\ 2 \\ \hline \end{array}$	48) $\begin{array}{r} 32 \\ \times\ 2 \\ \hline \end{array}$
49) $\begin{array}{r} 18 \\ \times\ 1 \\ \hline \end{array}$	50) $\begin{array}{r} 91 \\ \times\ 1 \\ \hline \end{array}$	51) $\begin{array}{r} 12 \\ \times\ 2 \\ \hline \end{array}$	52) $\begin{array}{r} 35 \\ \times\ 1 \\ \hline \end{array}$
53) $\begin{array}{r} 47 \\ \times\ 1 \\ \hline \end{array}$	54) $\begin{array}{r} 11 \\ \times\ 1 \\ \hline \end{array}$	55) $\begin{array}{r} 67 \\ \times\ 1 \\ \hline \end{array}$	56) $\begin{array}{r} 88 \\ \times\ 1 \\ \hline \end{array}$
57) $\begin{array}{r} 10 \\ \times\ 2 \\ \hline \end{array}$	58) $\begin{array}{r} 20 \\ \times\ 1 \\ \hline \end{array}$	59) $\begin{array}{r} 56 \\ \times\ 1 \\ \hline \end{array}$	60) $\begin{array}{r} 69 \\ \times\ 1 \\ \hline \end{array}$

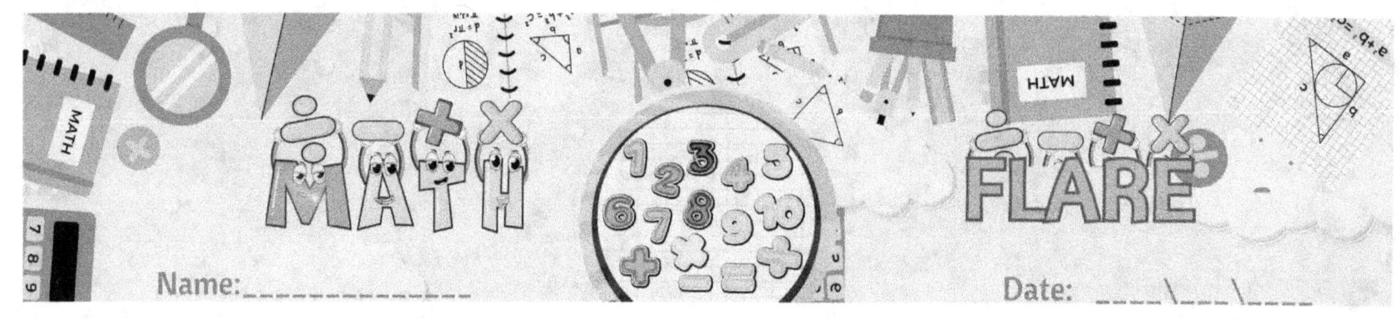

61) $\begin{array}{r} 15 \\ \times\ 1 \\ \hline \end{array}$	62) $\begin{array}{r} 44 \\ \times\ 1 \\ \hline \end{array}$	63) $\begin{array}{r} 89 \\ \times\ 1 \\ \hline \end{array}$	64) $\begin{array}{r} 77 \\ \times\ 1 \\ \hline \end{array}$
65) $\begin{array}{r} 57 \\ \times\ 1 \\ \hline \end{array}$	66) $\begin{array}{r} 26 \\ \times\ 1 \\ \hline \end{array}$	67) $\begin{array}{r} 43 \\ \times\ 1 \\ \hline \end{array}$	68) $\begin{array}{r} 59 \\ \times\ 1 \\ \hline \end{array}$
69) $\begin{array}{r} 50 \\ \times\ 1 \\ \hline \end{array}$	70) $\begin{array}{r} 32 \\ \times\ 1 \\ \hline \end{array}$	71) $\begin{array}{r} 92 \\ \times\ 1 \\ \hline \end{array}$	72) $\begin{array}{r} 39 \\ \times\ 1 \\ \hline \end{array}$
73) $\begin{array}{r} 70 \\ \times\ 1 \\ \hline \end{array}$	74) $\begin{array}{r} 81 \\ \times\ 1 \\ \hline \end{array}$	75) $\begin{array}{r} 42 \\ \times\ 1 \\ \hline \end{array}$	76) $\begin{array}{r} 19 \\ \times\ 1 \\ \hline \end{array}$
77) $\begin{array}{r} 71 \\ \times\ 1 \\ \hline \end{array}$	78) $\begin{array}{r} 72 \\ \times\ 1 \\ \hline \end{array}$	79) $\begin{array}{r} 17 \\ \times\ 1 \\ \hline \end{array}$	80) $\begin{array}{r} 66 \\ \times\ 1 \\ \hline \end{array}$

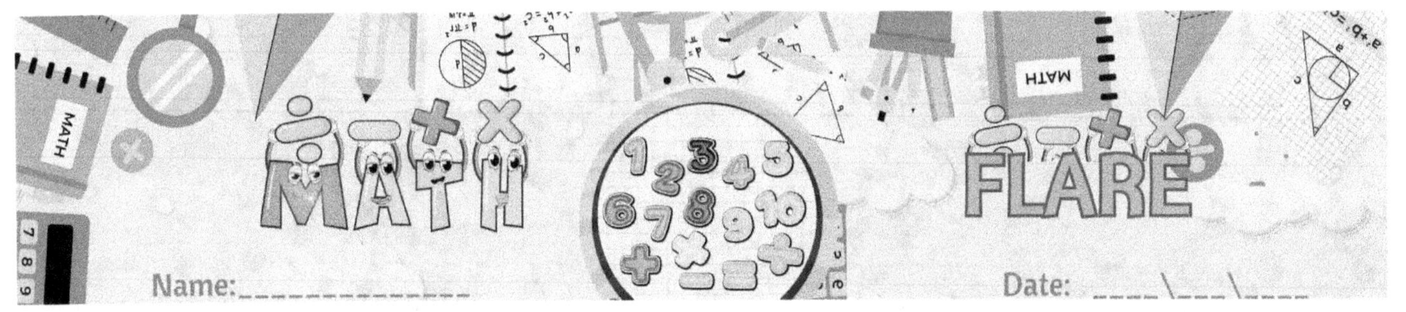

81) 53 × 1	82) 34 × 1	83) 46 × 1	84) 85 × 1
85) 13 × 1	86) 30 × 1	87) 95 × 1	88) 74 × 1
89) 37 × 1	90) 96 × 1	91) 97 × 1	92) 64 × 1
93) 93 × 1	94) 58 × 1	95) 75 × 1	96) 87 × 1
97) 45 × 1	98) 94 × 1	99) 16 × 1	100) 22 × 1

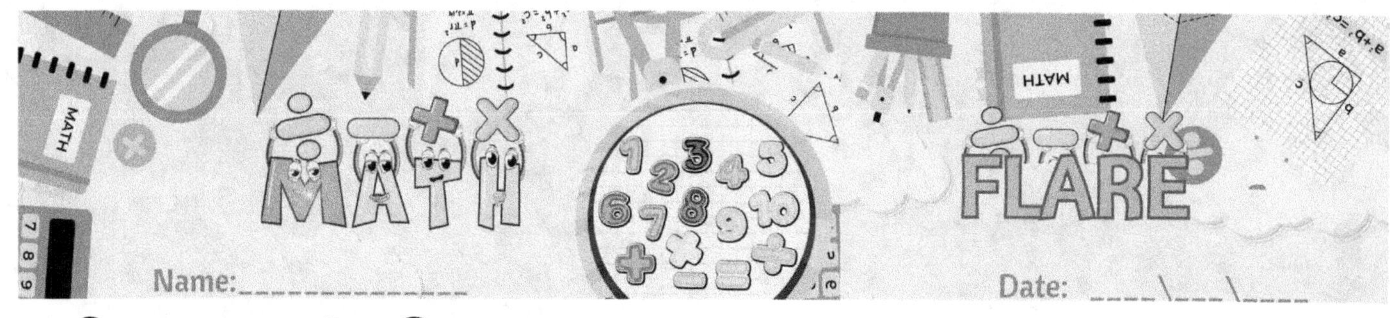

Commutative Property

Use the commutative property to fill the missing values.

1) $6 \times \underline{7} = 7 \times 6$

2) $8 \times 7 = \underline{} \times 8$

3) $1 \times 8 = \underline{} \times 1$

4) $9 \times 4 = \underline{} \times 9$

5) $9 \times 6 = 6 \times \underline{}$

6) $\underline{} \times 6 = 6 \times 4$

7) $2 \times 9 = \underline{} \times 2$

8) $4 + 2 = \underline{} + 4$

9) $\underline{} + 5 = 5 + 7$

10) $5 \times \underline{} = 4 \times 5$

11) $4 \times 3 = 3 \times \underline{}$

12) $2 \times \underline{} = 8 \times 2$

13) $6 \times \underline{} = 5 \times 6$

14) $7 + 9 = \underline{} + 7$

15) $5 + 3 = \underline{} + 5$

16) $7 + \underline{} = 3 + 7$

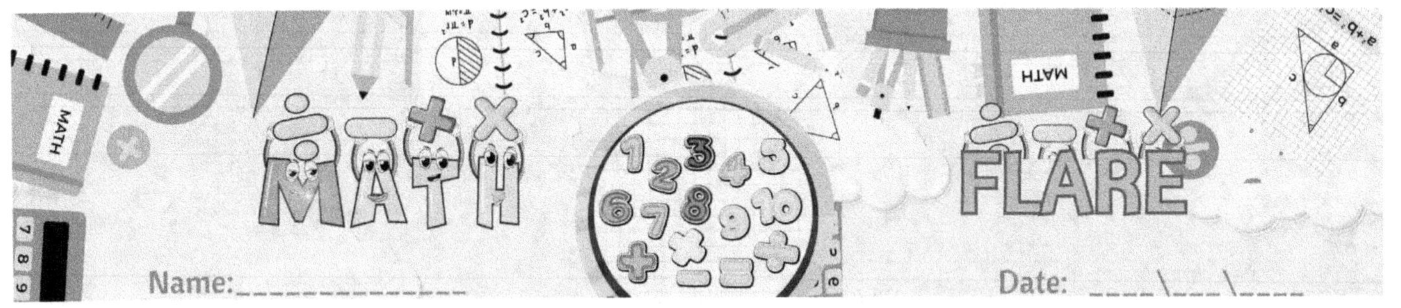

17) __ × 1 = 1 × 4

18) 10 + __ = 7 + 10

19) 10 + 1 = __ + 10

20) 8 × 3 = __ × 8

21) 9 × __ = 7 × 9

22) 7 × __ = 4 × 7

23) 5 × 6 = 6 × __

24) 2 × 3 = __ × 2

25) 5 × __ = 7 × 5

26) __ × 5 = 5 × 9

27) 3 × __ = 8 × 3

28) __ + 8 = 8 + 7

29) 7 × 10 = 10 × __

30) __ + 8 = 8 + 5

31) __ × 9 = 9 × 8

32) 8 × 1 = __ × 8

33) __ × 4 = 4 × 3

34) 3 + 10 = __ + 3

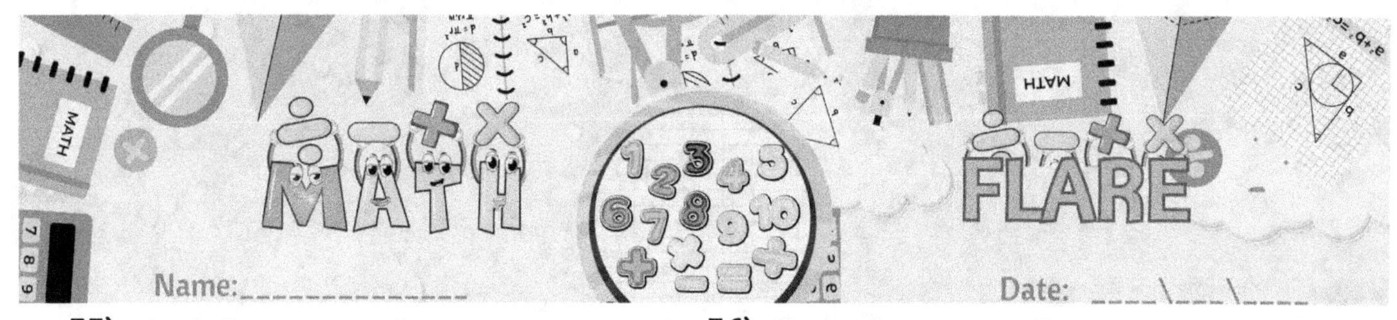

35) 4 × 9 = __ × 4

36) 3 + 6 = __ + 3

37) 8 + 2 = __ + 8

38) __ + 2 = 2 + 5

39) 1 + 6 = __ + 1

40) 4 × 8 = __ × 4

41) __ + 2 = 2 + 9

42) 2 + 4 = 4 + __

43) 9 × 3 = __ × 9

44) 4 × __ = 7 × 4

45) 5 × 1 = __ × 5

46) 3 + __ = 5 + 3

47) __ + 8 = 8 + 6

48) 7 × __ = 6 × 7

49) 6 + 3 = 3 + __

50) 2 × __ = 7 × 2

51) 10 × __ = 2 × 10

52) __ × 3 = 3 × 1

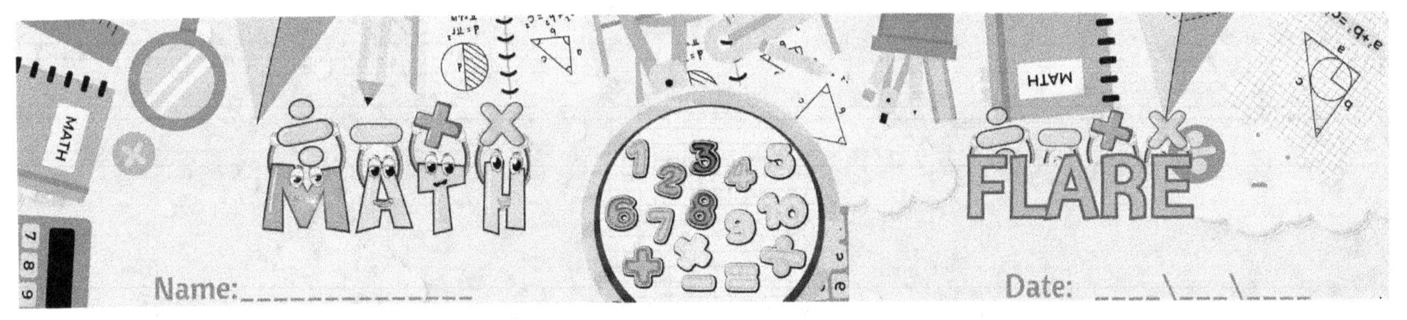

Division by 2

Find the quotient.

1)
$$\begin{array}{r} 5 \\ 2\overline{)10} \\ -10 \\ \hline 0 \end{array}$$

2)
$$\begin{array}{r} 18 \\ 2\overline{)36} \\ -2 \\ \hline 16 \\ -16 \\ \hline 0 \end{array}$$

3)
$$\begin{array}{r} 12 \\ 2\overline{)24} \\ -2 \\ \hline 04 \\ -4 \\ \hline 0 \end{array}$$

4)
$$\begin{array}{r} 14 \\ 2\overline{)28} \\ -2 \\ \hline 08 \\ -8 \\ \hline 0 \end{array}$$

5) $2\overline{)2}$

6) $2\overline{)6}$

7) $2\overline{)22}$

8) $2\overline{)32}$

9) $2\overline{)34}$

10) $2\overline{)8}$

11) $2\overline{)4}$

12) $2\overline{)12}$

13) $2\overline{)18}$

14) $2\overline{)14}$

15) $2\overline{)26}$

16) $2\overline{)38}$

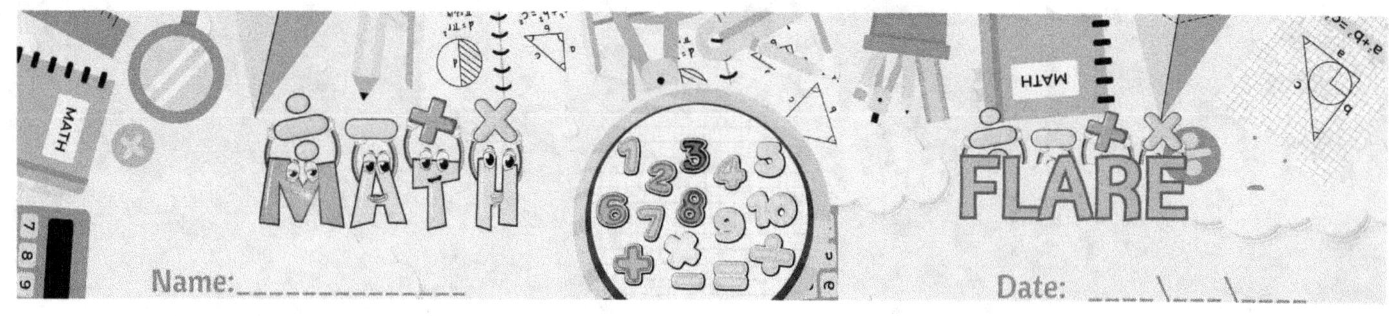

Division by 3

Find the quotient.

1) $3\overline{)6}$

2) $3\overline{)30}$

3) $3\overline{)18}$

4) $3\overline{)9}$

5) $3\overline{)27}$

6) $3\overline{)24}$

7) $3\overline{)3}$

8) $3\overline{)15}$

9) $3\overline{)21}$

10) $3\overline{)12}$

11) $3\overline{)6}$

12) $3\overline{)9}$

13) $3\overline{)21}$

14) $3\overline{)9}$

15) $3\overline{)21}$

16) $3\overline{)27}$

17) $3\overline{)27}$

18) $3\overline{)27}$

19) $3\overline{)6}$

20) $3\overline{)21}$

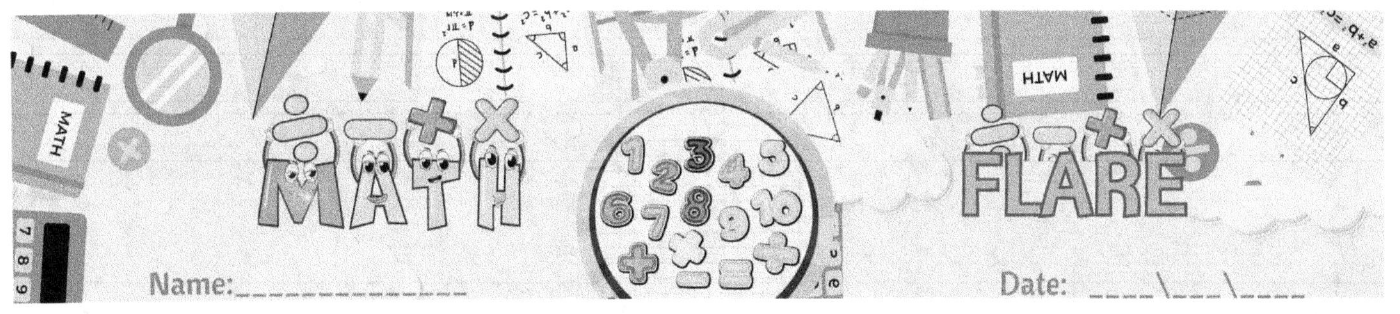

Division by 4

Find the quotient.

1) $4\overline{)36}$

2) $4\overline{)8}$

3) $4\overline{)20}$

4) $4\overline{)16}$

5) $4\overline{)32}$

6) $4\overline{)28}$

7) $4\overline{)12}$

8) $4\overline{)40}$

9) $4\overline{)24}$

10) $4\overline{)4}$

11) $4\overline{)28}$

12) $4\overline{)32}$

13) $4\overline{)16}$

14) $4\overline{)36}$

15) $4\overline{)16}$

16) $4\overline{)28}$

17) $4\overline{)36}$

18) $4\overline{)20}$

19) $4\overline{)8}$

20) $4\overline{)16}$

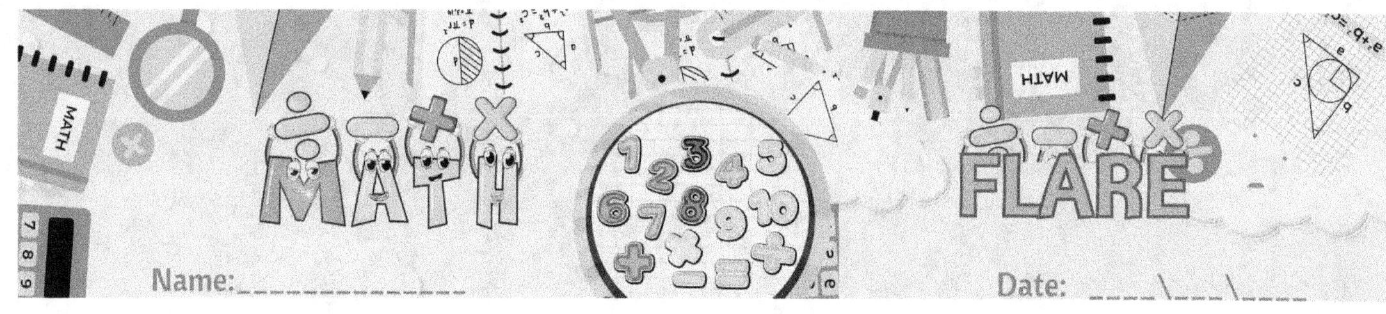

Division by 5

Find the quotient.

1) $5\overline{)35}$

2) $5\overline{)30}$

3) $5\overline{)25}$

4) $5\overline{)10}$

5) $5\overline{)20}$

6) $5\overline{)50}$

7) $5\overline{)15}$

8) $5\overline{)45}$

9) $5\overline{)40}$

10) $5\overline{)5}$

11) $5\overline{)15}$

12) $5\overline{)45}$

13) $5\overline{)30}$

14) $5\overline{)15}$

15) $5\overline{)45}$

16) $5\overline{)30}$

17) $5\overline{)50}$

18) $5\overline{)10}$

19) $5\overline{)35}$

20) $5\overline{)30}$

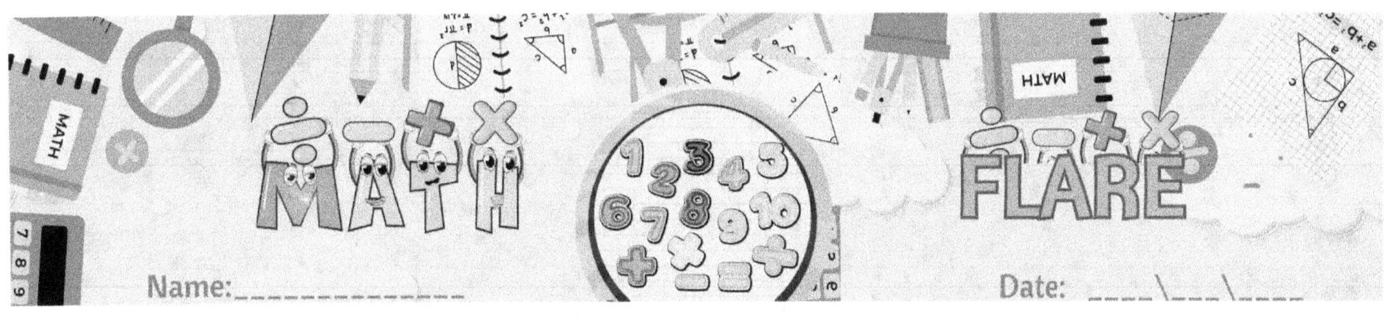

Division by 6

Find the quotient.

1) $6\overline{)18}$
2) $6\overline{)36}$
3) $6\overline{)60}$
4) $6\overline{)30}$

5) $6\overline{)12}$
6) $6\overline{)42}$
7) $6\overline{)6}$
8) $6\overline{)48}$

9) $6\overline{)24}$
10) $6\overline{)54}$
11) $6\overline{)36}$
12) $6\overline{)12}$

13) $6\overline{)42}$
14) $6\overline{)18}$
15) $6\overline{)54}$
16) $6\overline{)30}$

17) $6\overline{)54}$
18) $6\overline{)54}$
19) $6\overline{)12}$
20) $6\overline{)30}$

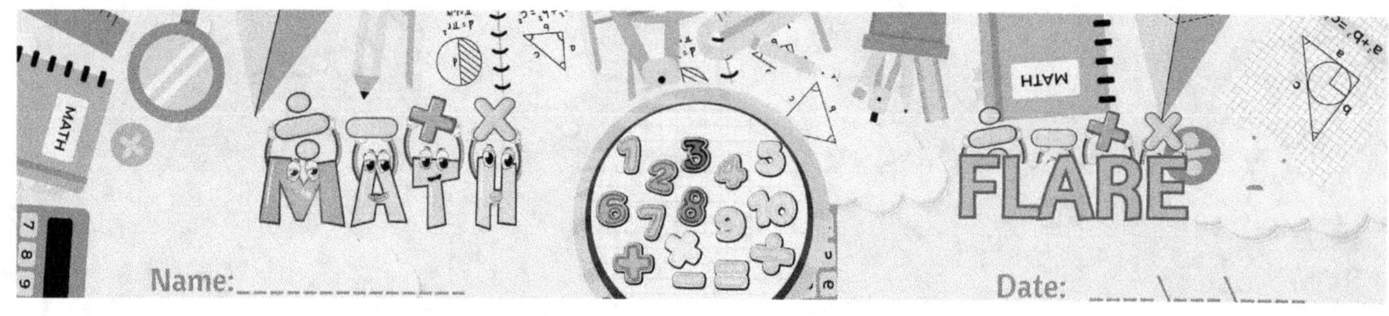

Division by 7

Find the quotient.

1) 7)28

2) 7)56

3) 7)49

4) 7)63

5) 7)42

6) 7)70

7) 7)35

8) 7)21

9) 7)7

10) 7)14

11) 7)49

12) 7)49

13) 7)63

14) 7)42

15) 7)35

16) 7)14

17) 7)35

18) 7)42

19) 7)35

20) 7)21

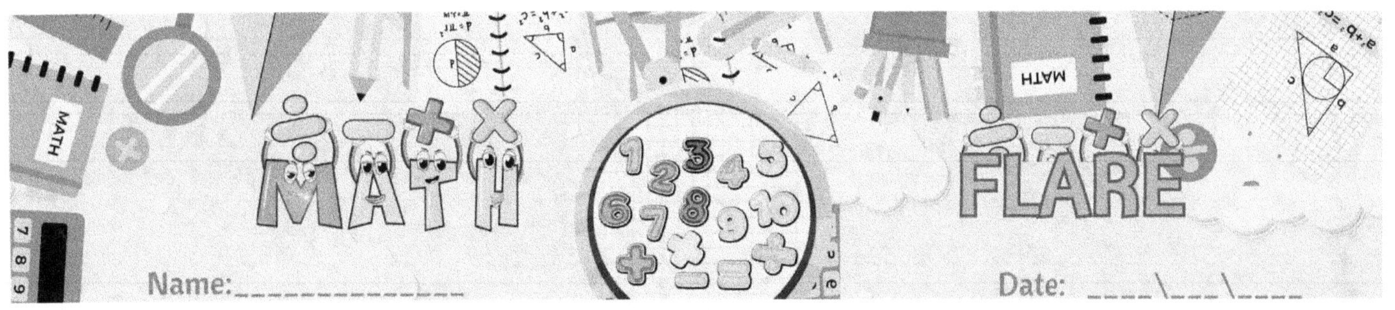

Division by 8

Find the quotient.

1)   8)40

2)   8)8

3)   8)32

4)   8)64

5)   8)80

6)   8)72

7)   8)56

8)   8)16

9)   8)24

10)   8)48

11)   8)40

12)   8)64

13)   8)24

14)   8)8

15)   8)56

16)   8)16

17)   8)16

18)   8)56

19)   8)56

20)   8)24

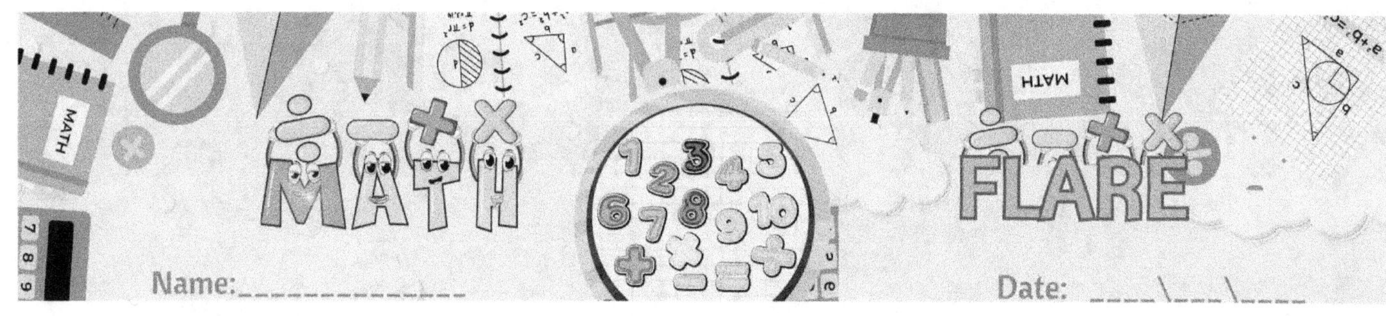

Division by 9

Find the quotient.

1) $9\overline{)81}$ 2) $9\overline{)18}$ 3) $9\overline{)54}$ 4) $9\overline{)72}$

5) $9\overline{)9}$ 6) $9\overline{)45}$ 7) $9\overline{)27}$ 8) $9\overline{)36}$

9) $9\overline{)63}$ 10) $9\overline{)90}$ 11) $9\overline{)72}$ 12) $9\overline{)72}$

13) $9\overline{)18}$ 14) $9\overline{)18}$ 15) $9\overline{)63}$ 16) $9\overline{)27}$

17) $9\overline{)18}$ 18) $9\overline{)18}$ 19) $9\overline{)27}$ 20) $9\overline{)45}$

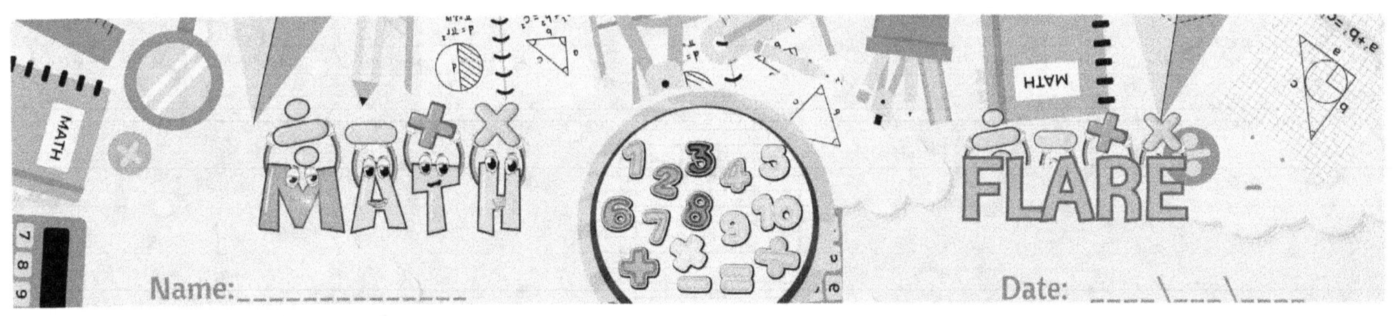

Division by 10

Find the quotient.

1) $10\overline{)100}$

2) $10\overline{)50}$

3) $10\overline{)30}$

4) $10\overline{)110}$

5) $10\overline{)70}$

6) $10\overline{)160}$

7) $10\overline{)10}$

8) $10\overline{)170}$

9) $10\overline{)150}$

10) $10\overline{)120}$

11) $10\overline{)200}$

12) $10\overline{)80}$

13) $10\overline{)60}$

14) $10\overline{)90}$

15) $10\overline{)180}$

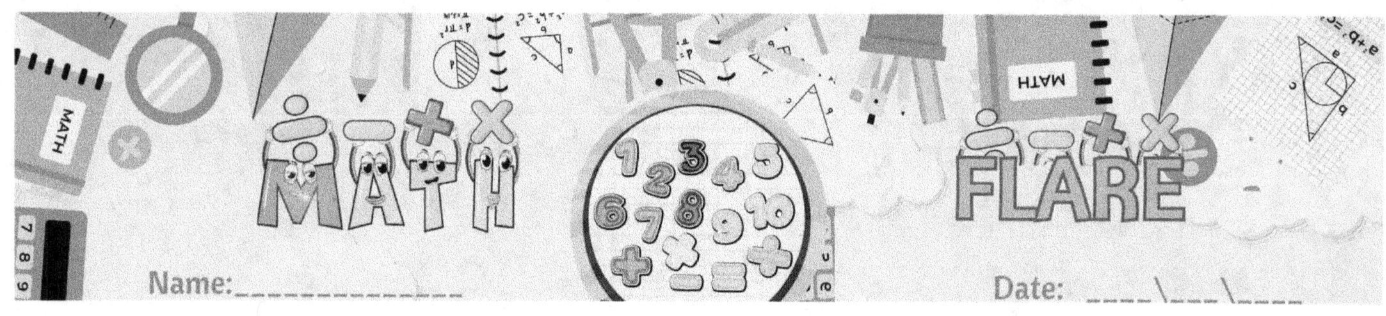

Basic Division

Find the quotient.

1)   6)‾36

2)   6)‾66

3)   4)‾44

4)   6)‾30

5)   1)‾20

6)   2)‾38

7)   8)‾56

8)   6)‾54

9)   10)‾130

10)   2)‾34

11)   1)‾10

12)   6)‾108

13)   9)‾18

14)   8)‾72

15)   9)‾27

16)   1)‾11

17)   4)‾20

18)   8)‾8

19)   10)‾150

20)   4)‾48

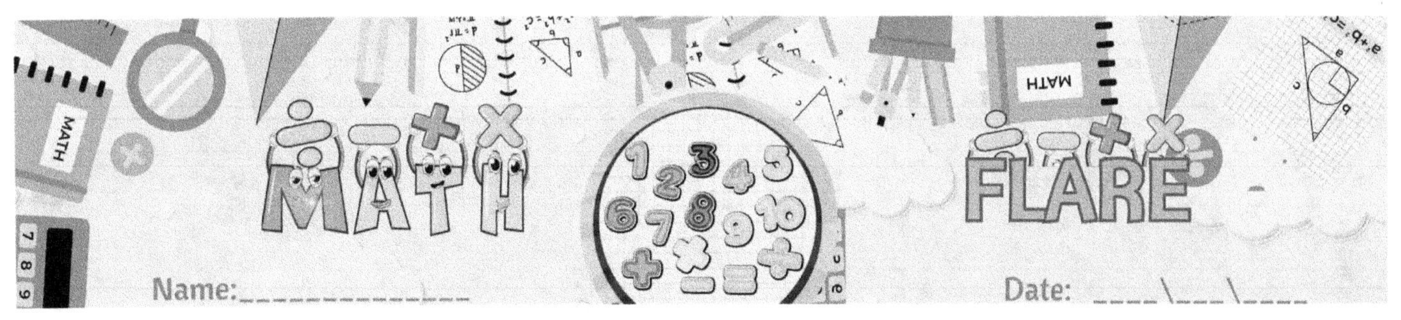

21)

3)36

22)

3)33

23)

4)76

24)

8)40

25)

5)20

26)

2)28

27)

8)104

28)

7)35

29)

8)16

30)

1)2

31)

9)54

32)

10)80

33)

7)133

34)

7)56

35)

3)54

36)

7)49

37)

8)136

38)

5)80

39)

9)63

40)

4)60

41) $6\overline{)24}$

42) $6\overline{)18}$

43) $10\overline{)90}$

44) $2\overline{)20}$

45) $9\overline{)153}$

46) $1\overline{)7}$

47) $5\overline{)95}$

48) $5\overline{)15}$

49) $2\overline{)24}$

50) $7\overline{)98}$

51) $9\overline{)99}$

52) $6\overline{)120}$

53) $5\overline{)35}$

54) $4\overline{)36}$

55) $9\overline{)45}$

56) $4\overline{)12}$

57) $3\overline{)9}$

58) $5\overline{)65}$

59) $2\overline{)2}$

60) $3\overline{)57}$

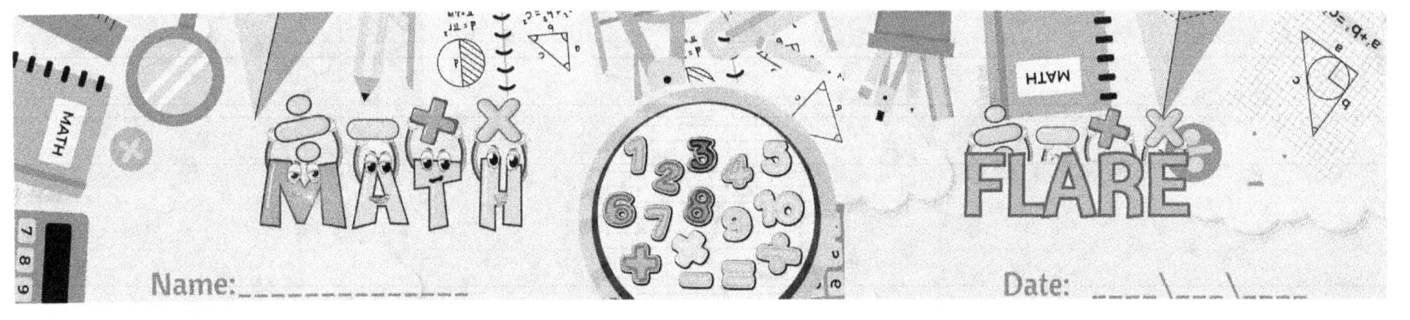

61)

$9\overline{)81}$

62)

$5\overline{)30}$

63)

$6\overline{)12}$

64)

$9\overline{)90}$

65)

$4\overline{)68}$

66)

$6\overline{)96}$

67)

$5\overline{)60}$

68)

$6\overline{)102}$

69)

$2\overline{)10}$

70)

$10\overline{)200}$

71)

$5\overline{)55}$

72)

$4\overline{)24}$

73)

$8\overline{)80}$

74)

$5\overline{)50}$

75)

$4\overline{)56}$

76)

$1\overline{)17}$

77)

$6\overline{)72}$

78)

$5\overline{)40}$

79)

$9\overline{)117}$

80)

$6\overline{)114}$

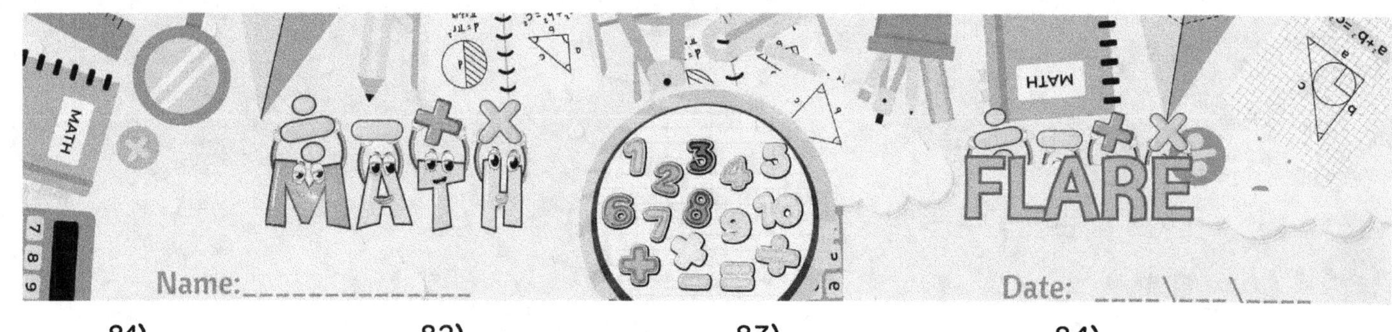

81) $10\overline{)70}$

82) $7\overline{)126}$

83) $4\overline{)32}$

84) $7\overline{)77}$

85) $10\overline{)140}$

86) $2\overline{)16}$

87) $7\overline{)119}$

88) $8\overline{)48}$

89) $6\overline{)42}$

90) $7\overline{)91}$

91) $2\overline{)36}$

92) $3\overline{)48}$

93) $2\overline{)12}$

94) $4\overline{)16}$

95) $10\overline{)60}$

96) $3\overline{)51}$

97) $3\overline{)21}$

98) $8\overline{)152}$

99) $2\overline{)22}$

100) $8\overline{)88}$

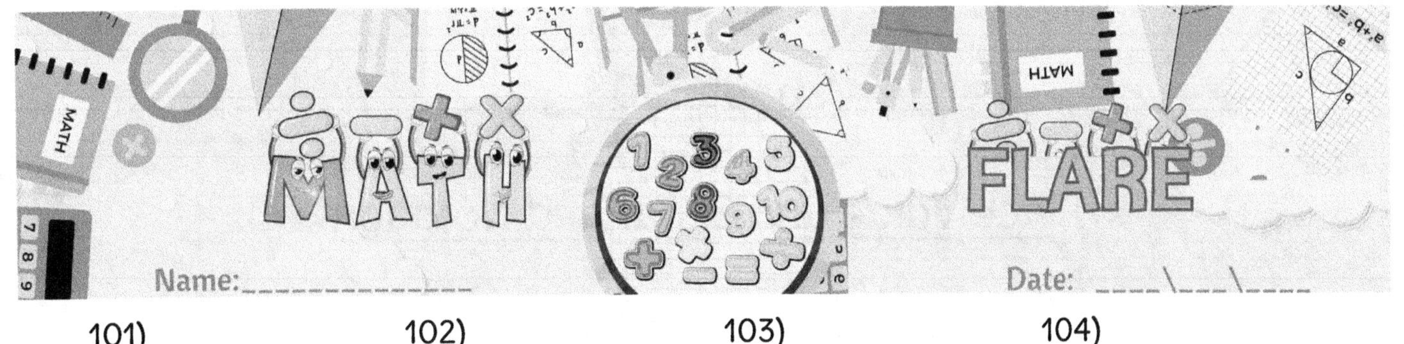

101)
$2\overline{)32}$

102)
$7\overline{)63}$

103)
$3\overline{)30}$

104)
$4\overline{)40}$

105)
$9\overline{)171}$

106)
$3\overline{)39}$

107)
$3\overline{)60}$

108)
$7\overline{)105}$

109)
$5\overline{)10}$

110)
$10\overline{)180}$

111)
$4\overline{)64}$

112)
$2\overline{)30}$

113)
$9\overline{)144}$

114)
$9\overline{)108}$

115)
$1\overline{)16}$

116)
$9\overline{)72}$

117)
$9\overline{)180}$

118)
$2\overline{)4}$

119)
$6\overline{)78}$

120)
$3\overline{)27}$

Chapter. 03

Place Value and Expanded Notation

Place value tells us the value of a digit in a number based on where it's placed.

Imagine we have the number 45,643. It has five digits: 4, 5, 6, 4, and 3.

Now, each digit holds a special place. Let's break down the number 45,643:

- The first digit, 4, is in the ten thousands place.

- The second digit, 5, is in the thousands place.

- The third digit, 6, is in the hundreds place.

- The fourth digit, 4, is in the tens place.

- The fifth digit, 3, is in the ones place.

When we add these values together, we find the value of the entire number:

$$40000 + 5000 + 600 + 40 + 3 = 45,643$$

Expanded notation helps us see the individual value of each digit in a number and how they contribute to the overall value of the number. It's like breaking down a big puzzle into smaller pieces to understand it better!

So, in expanded notation, we can write 45,643 as: 40000 (from ten thousand place) + 5000 (from thousands place) + 600 (from the hundreds place) + 40 (from the tens place) + 3 (from the ones place).

Let's solve problems from exercises:

Place value of the underline digit:

$$85{,}644 = \underline{\text{5 thousands}}$$

Expanded notations:

$\underline{63{,}698}$ 6 ten thousands + 3 thousands + 6 hundreds + 9 tens + 8 ones

15,643   1 ten thousand + 5 thousands + 6 hundreds + 4 tens + 3 ones

$\underline{64{,}612}$ $60{,}000 + 4{,}000 + 600 + 10 + 2$

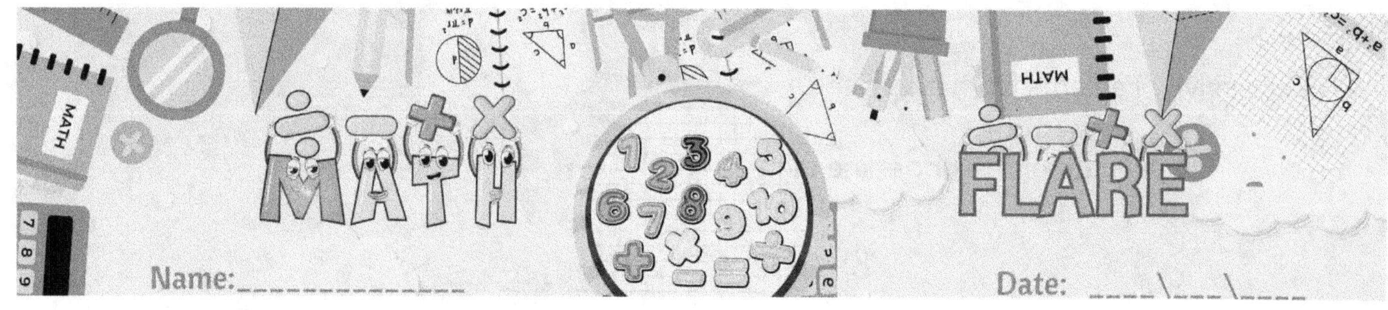

Place Value

Determine the place value of the underlined digit.

1) 85,644 = _5 thousands_

2) 82,201 = _______________

3) 15,731 = _______________

4) 78,385 = _______________

5) 77,490 = _______________

6) 71,883 = _______________

7) 29,769 = _______________

8) 99,176 = _______________

9) 26,849 = _______________

10) 89,045 = _______________

11) 87,359 = _______________

12) 67,156 = _______________

13) 51,028 = _______________

14) 71,850 = _______________

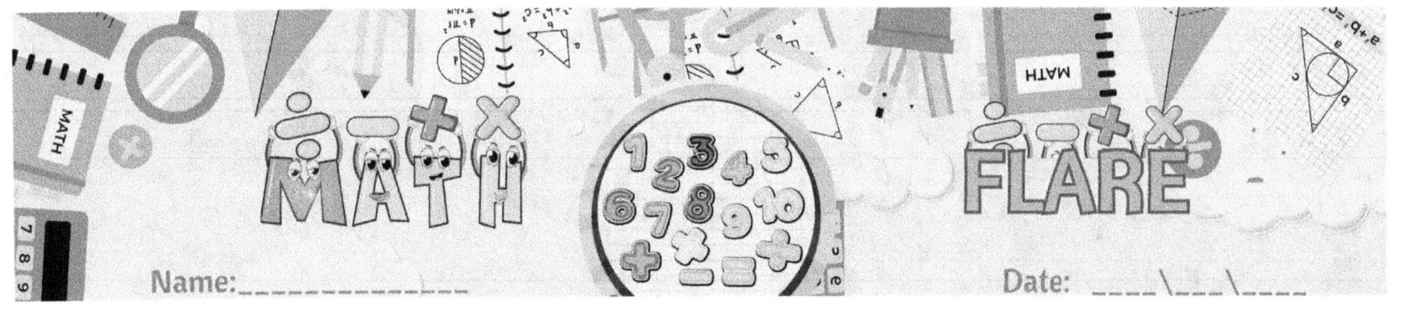

15) 17,319 = _______________

16) 45,939 = _______________

17) 82,200 = _______________

18) 68,702 = _______________

19) 63,783 = _______________

20) 64,770 = _______________

21) 94,966 = _______________

22) 30,844 = _______________

23) 65,931 = _______________

24) 94,759 = _______________

25) 44,347 = _______________

26) 92,408 = _______________

27) 46,380 = _______________

28) 25,794 = _______________

29) 41,970 = _______________

30) 44,404 = _______________

31) <u>8</u>8,758 = _______________

32) <u>7</u>1,931 = _______________

33) 77,23<u>8</u> = _______________

34) 45,99<u>7</u> = _______________

35) <u>2</u>3,391 = _______________

36) <u>5</u>2,550 = _______________

37) <u>5</u>5,630 = _______________

38) 1<u>4</u>,221 = _______________

39) 69,<u>4</u>79 = _______________

40) 51,<u>7</u>25 = _______________

41) 86,<u>6</u>07 = _______________

42) 64,49<u>2</u> = _______________

43) <u>5</u>2,209 = _______________

44) 36,<u>6</u>98 = _______________

45) 1<u>3</u>,990 = _______________

46) 59,1<u>6</u>3 = _______________

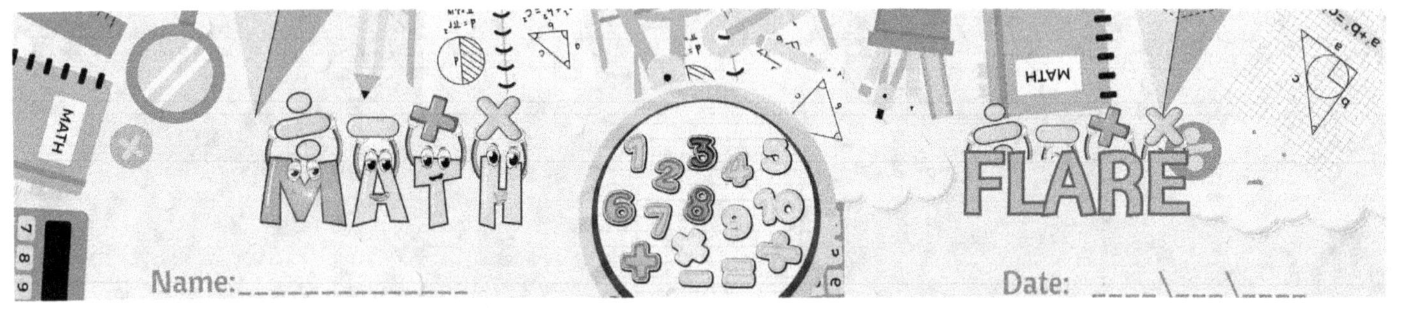

47) 69,9<u>5</u>7 = ___________________

48) <u>7</u>2,279 = ___________________

49) <u>6</u>6,673 = ___________________

50) 6<u>7</u>,457 = ___________________

51) 54,<u>0</u>94 = ___________________

52) <u>7</u>3,515 = ___________________

53) <u>6</u>6,437 = ___________________

54) 62,8<u>8</u>3 = ___________________

55) 54,5<u>8</u>3 = ___________________

56) 64,80<u>0</u> = ___________________

57) <u>2</u>6,271 = ___________________

58) 20,9<u>7</u>1 = ___________________

59) 44,<u>0</u>38 = ___________________

60) 85,<u>0</u>81 = ___________________

61) 35,<u>5</u>03 = ___________________

62) 13,<u>9</u>75 = ___________________

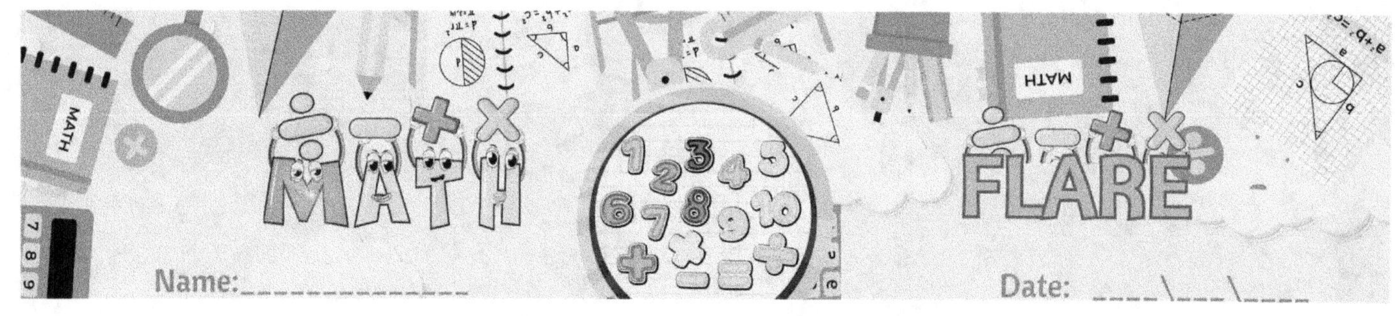

63) 67,20<u>6</u> = _______________

64) 82,4<u>4</u>4 = _______________

65) 10,2<u>8</u>7 = _______________

66) 25,4<u>2</u>8 = _______________

67) 8<u>9</u>,916 = _______________

68) 15,03<u>1</u> = _______________

69) <u>5</u>8,460 = _______________

70) 64,76<u>8</u> = _______________

71) 90,30<u>9</u> = _______________

72) 77,9<u>7</u>8 = _______________

73) 99,<u>2</u>22 = _______________

74) 2<u>2</u>,058 = _______________

75) 78,16<u>2</u> = _______________

76) 40,47<u>4</u> = _______________

77) 78,63<u>4</u> = _______________

78) 39,<u>2</u>33 = _______________

79) 90,769 = _________________

80) 85,183 = _________________

81) 32,451 = _________________

82) 74,100 = _________________

83) 59,120 = _________________

84) 74,513 = _________________

85) 90,310 = _________________

86) 25,243 = _________________

87) 15,494 = _________________

88) 24,356 = _________________

89) 91,413 = _________________

90) 58,590 = _________________

91) 36,279 = _________________

92) 44,659 = _________________

93) 70,182 = _________________

94) 84,397 = _________________

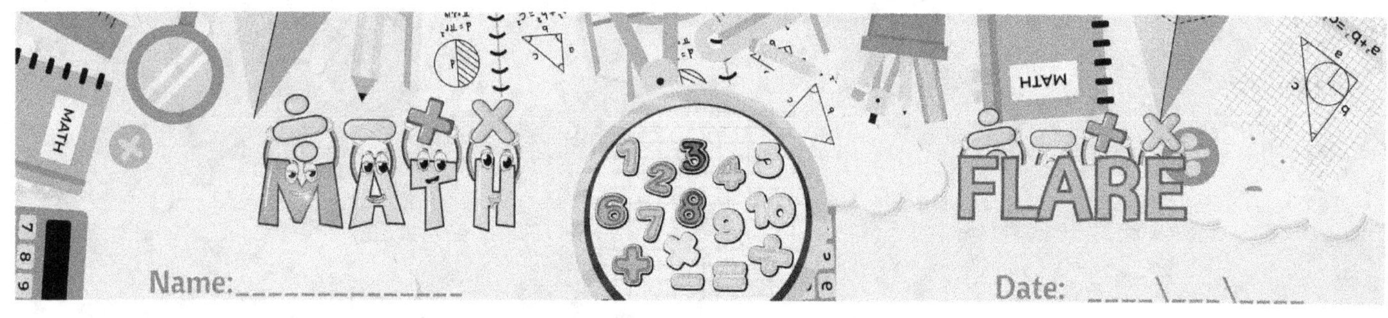

Place Value: Expanded Notation

Provide the expanded notation for each value.

1) ____63,698____ 6 ten thousands + 3 thousands + 6 hundreds + 9 tens + 8 ones

2) ____________ 4 ten thousands + 1 hundred + 3 tens + 9 ones

3) ____________ 1 ten thousand + 9 thousands + 2 hundreds + 6 tens + 7 ones

4) ____________ 9 ten thousands + 9 thousands + 6 hundreds + 9 tens

5) ____________ 1 ten thousand + 7 thousands + 2 hundreds + 7 tens + 4 ones

6) ____________ 2 ten thousands + 9 thousands + 8 hundreds + 9 ones

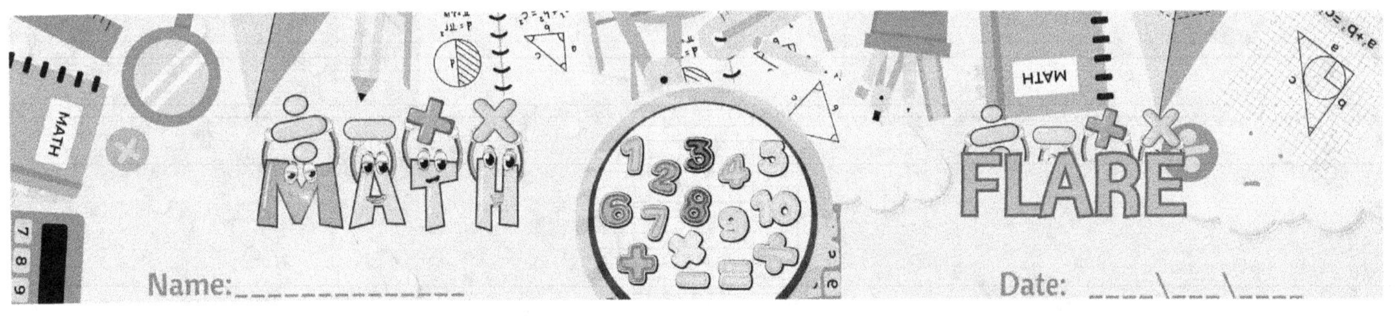

7) _________________ 5 ten thousands + 7 thousands + 7 hundreds + 5 tens + 8 ones

8) _________________ 1 ten thousand + 4 thousands + 9 hundreds + 9 tens + 6 ones

9) _________________ 8 ten thousands + 6 thousands + 5 hundreds + 3 ones

10) _________________ 8 ten thousands + 4 thousands + 1 hundred + 6 tens + 8 ones

11) _________________ 9 ten thousands + 3 hundreds + 6 ones

12) _________________ 7 ten thousands + 1 thousand + 8 hundreds + 5 tens

13) _________________ 6 ten thousands + 6 thousands + 4 hundreds + 1 ten

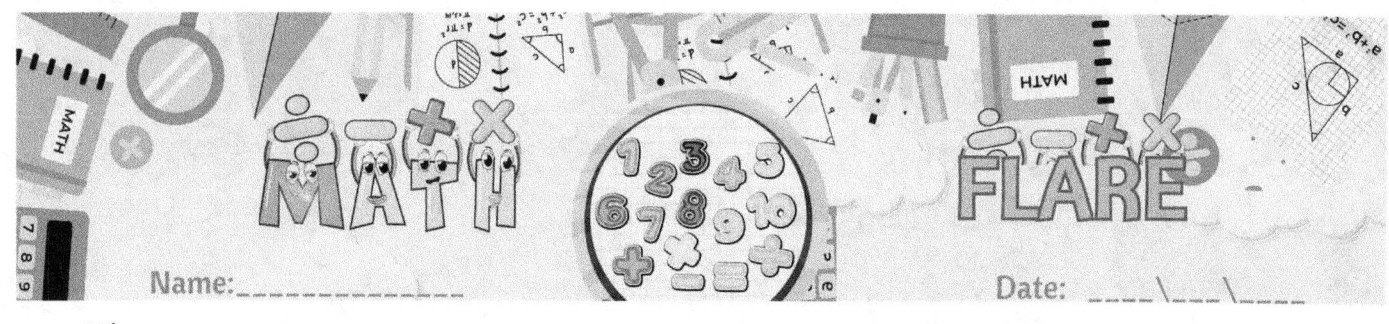

14) _________________ 2 ten thousands + 7 thousands + 5 hundreds + 2 tens + 9 ones

15) _________________ 3 ten thousands + 1 thousand + 4 hundreds + 3 tens + 9 ones

16) _________________ 5 ten thousands + 2 thousands + 3 hundreds + 2 tens + 9 ones

17) _________________ 4 ten thousands + 6 thousands + 5 tens + 7 ones

18) _________________ 3 ten thousands + 2 thousands + 7 hundreds + 6 tens

19) _________________ 9 ten thousands + 4 thousands + 4 hundreds + 1 ten + 1 one

20) _________________ 2 ten thousands + 6 hundreds + 6 tens + 5 ones

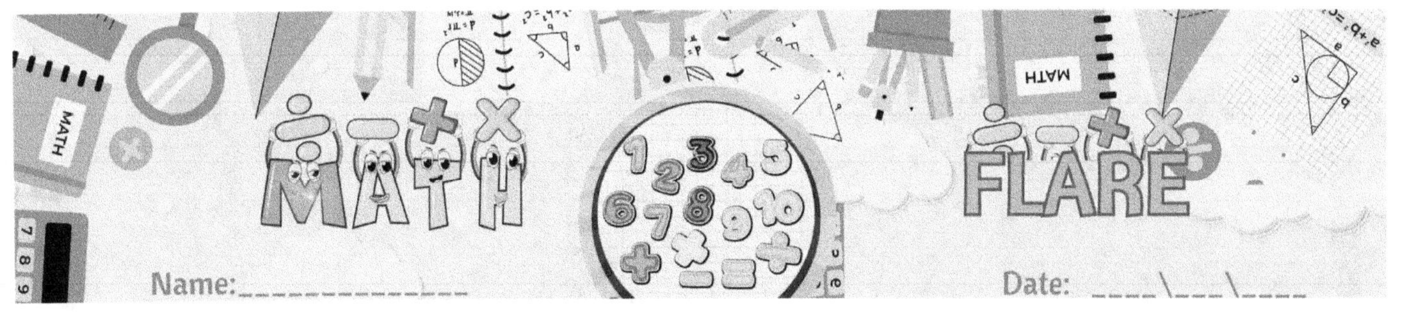

21) _________________ 7 ten thousands + 8 thousands + 8 hundreds + 8 tens + 7 ones

22) _________________ 6 ten thousands + 4 thousands + 7 hundreds + 9 tens

23) _________________ 2 ten thousands + 3 thousands + 8 hundreds + 3 tens + 9 ones

24) _________________ 2 ten thousands + 9 thousands + 4 hundreds + 5 tens + 8 ones

25) _________________ 3 ten thousands + 2 thousands + 6 tens + 3 ones

26) _________________ 5 ten thousands + 2 thousands + 6 hundreds + 1 ten

27) _________________ 5 ten thousands + 6 thousands + 2 hundreds + 4 tens + 7 ones

28) _________________ 9 ten thousands + 5 thousands + 4 hundreds +
8 tens + 1 one

29) _________________ 4 ten thousands + 9 thousands + 9 hundreds +
2 tens + 9 ones

30) _________________ 4 ten thousands + 2 thousands + 3 hundreds +
1 ten + 8 ones

31) _________________ 3 ten thousands + 4 thousands + 2 hundreds +
2 tens + 1 one

32) _________________ 4 ten thousands + 4 thousands + 7 hundreds +
2 tens + 4 ones

33) _________________ 2 ten thousands + 8 thousands + 5 tens + 8
ones

34) _________________ 6 ten thousands + 6 thousands + 3 hundreds +
9 tens + 4 ones

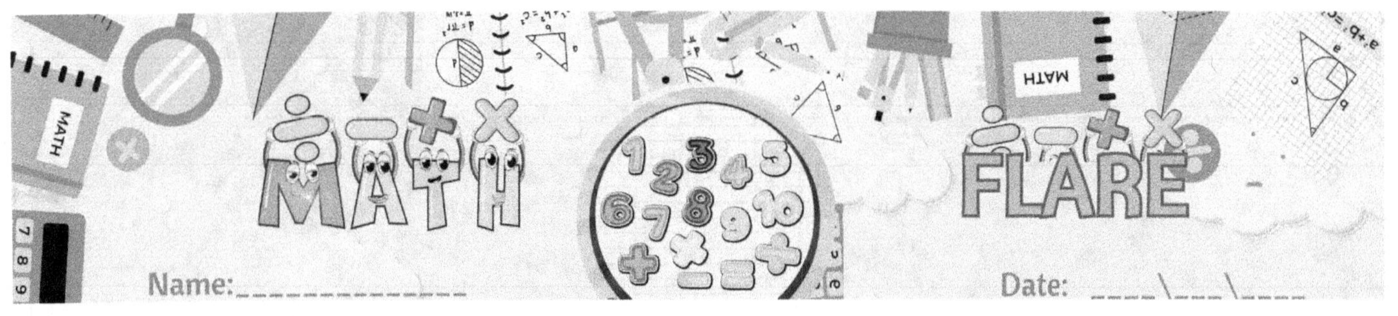

35) _________________ 7 ten thousands + 7 thousands + 3 hundreds + 1 ten + 6 ones

36) _________________ 3 ten thousands + 7 thousands + 6 hundreds + 1 ten + 1 one

37) _________________ 2 ten thousands + 9 thousands + 3 hundreds + 2 tens + 5 ones

38) _________________ 4 ten thousands + 1 thousand + 5 hundreds + 4 tens + 7 ones

39) _________________ 5 ten thousands + 4 thousands + 1 hundred + 8 tens + 1 one

40) _________________ 1 ten thousand + 3 thousands + 7 hundreds + 7 tens + 1 one

41) _________________ 7 ten thousands + 4 thousands + 4 hundreds + 9 tens + 3 ones

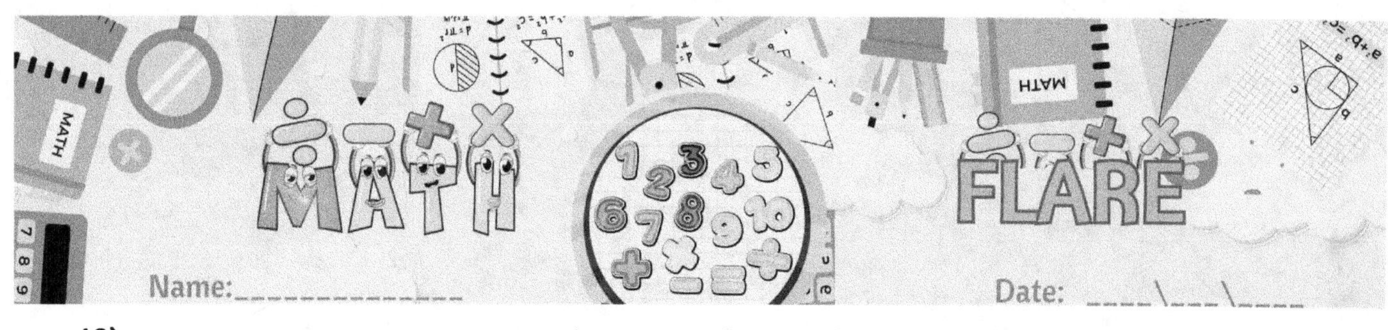

42) _________________ 2 ten thousands + 1 thousand + 2 hundreds + 2 tens + 1 one

43) _________________ 5 ten thousands + 9 thousands + 8 hundreds + 2 tens + 7 ones

44) _________________ 9 ten thousands + 9 thousands + 6 hundreds + 3 tens + 1 one

45) _________________ 8 ten thousands + 5 thousands + 5 hundreds + 6 tens + 1 one

46) _________________ 8 ten thousands + 4 thousands + 2 tens + 5 ones

47) _________________ 3 ten thousands + 5 thousands + 7 tens + 1 one

48) _________________ 8 ten thousands + 5 thousands + 4 tens + 1 one

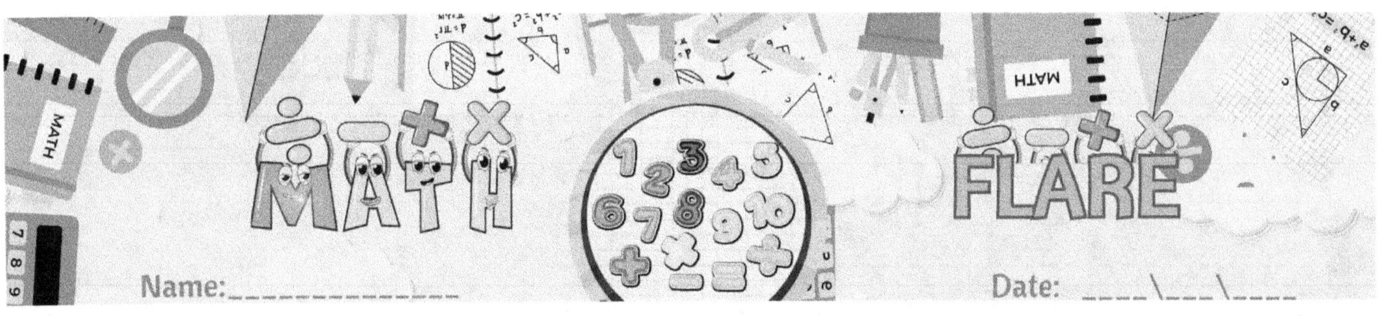

49) _______________ 2 ten thousands + 9 thousands + 4 ones

50) _______________ 5 ten thousands + 4 thousands + 5 tens + 3 ones

51) _______________ 5 ten thousands + 9 thousands + 7 tens

52) _______________ 4 ten thousands + 2 thousands + 2 hundreds + 6 tens + 5 ones

53) _______________ 1 ten thousand + 2 thousands + 5 tens + 4 ones

54) _______________ 6 ten thousands + 7 thousands + 7 hundreds + 4 tens + 4 ones

55) _______________ 5 ten thousands + 7 thousands + 7 hundreds + 7 tens + 4 ones

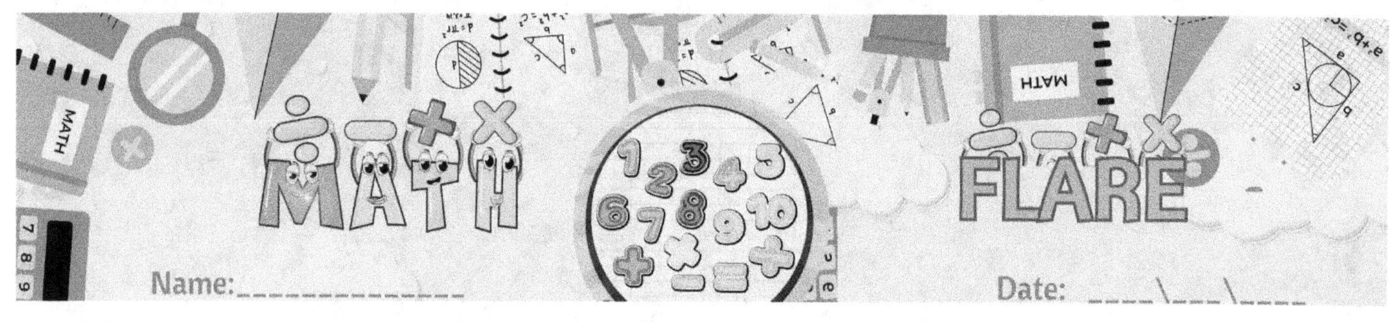

56) _________________ 9 ten thousands + 8 thousands + 9 hundreds + 7 ones

57) _________________ 2 ten thousands + 6 thousands + 3 hundreds + 1 one

58) _________________ 8 ten thousands + 9 thousands + 8 hundreds + 8 ones

59) _________________ 7 ten thousands + 7 thousands + 6 hundreds + 2 tens + 8 ones

60) _________________ 6 ten thousands + 4 thousands + 6 hundreds + 6 tens + 3 ones

61) _________________ 7 ten thousands + 3 thousands + 5 hundreds + 6 tens

62) _________________ 6 ten thousands + 2 thousands + 2 hundreds + 7 tens + 6 ones

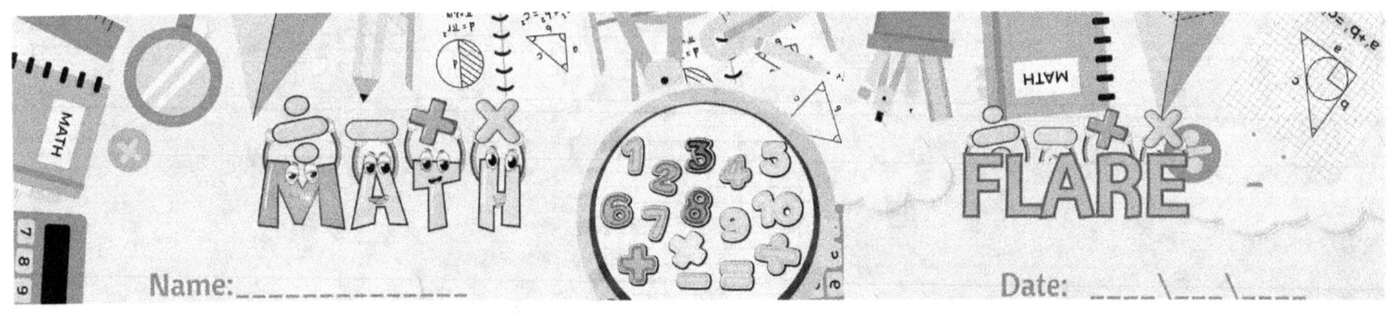

63) _________________ 6 ten thousands + 5 thousands + 6 tens + 6 ones

64) _________________ 5 ten thousands + 4 thousands + 1 hundred + 8 tens + 4 ones

65) _________________ 5 ten thousands + 9 thousands + 9 hundreds + 4 tens + 6 ones

66) _________________ 5 ten thousands + 5 thousands + 5 hundreds + 8 tens + 1 one

67) _________________ 5 ten thousands + 3 thousands + 7 hundreds + 9 tens + 2 ones

68) _________________ 1 ten thousand + 1 ten + 6 ones

69) _________________ 5 ten thousands + 2 hundreds + 1 ten + 2 ones

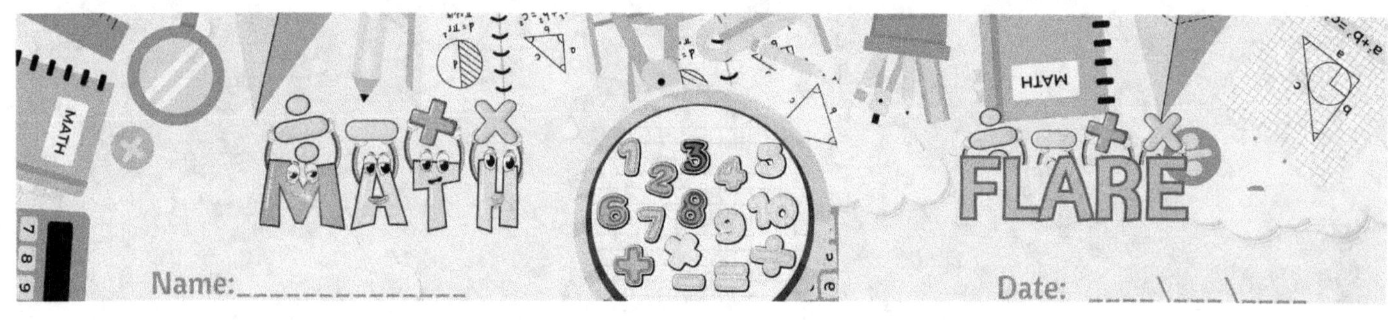

70) _________________ 9 ten thousands + 3 thousands + 8 hundreds + 2 tens + 7 ones

71) _________________ 3 ten thousands + 3 thousands + 3 ones

72) _________________ 1 ten thousand + 4 thousands + 5 hundreds + 1 ten

73) _________________ 7 ten thousands + 8 thousands + 5 hundreds + 7 tens + 8 ones

74) _________________ 9 ten thousands + 6 hundreds + 4 tens

75) _________________ 4 ten thousands + 6 thousands + 1 hundred + 7 tens + 1 one

76) _________________ 6 ten thousands + 7 thousands + 6 hundreds + 6 tens + 7 ones

77) _________________ 1 ten thousand + 4 thousands + 9 hundreds + 6 tens + 2 ones

78) _________________ 2 ten thousands + 4 thousands + 2 hundreds + 7 ones

79) _________________ 4 ten thousands + 3 thousands + 8 hundreds + 9 tens + 6 ones

80) _________________ 4 ten thousands + 8 thousands + 3 tens + 7 ones

81) _________________ 2 ten thousands + 7 thousands + 5 hundreds + 3 tens + 9 ones

82) _________________ 7 ten thousands + 1 thousand + 2 hundreds + 6 ones

83) _________________ 7 ten thousands + 6 thousands + 4 hundreds + 7 tens + 7 ones

Name:____________________ Date: ____________

84) ______________ 9 ten thousands + 5 thousands + 8 hundreds +
7 tens + 5 ones

85) ______________ 8 ten thousands + 3 thousands + 2 hundreds +
4 tens + 7 ones

86) ______________ 9 ten thousands + 1 thousand + 9 hundreds + 5
tens + 5 ones

87) ______________ 4 ten thousands + 2 thousands + 6 hundreds +
7 tens

88) ______________ 6 ten thousands + 3 hundreds + 1 ten + 4 ones

89) ______________ 1 ten thousand + 8 thousands + 6 hundreds + 2
tens

90) ______________ 7 ten thousands + 8 thousands + 4 hundreds +
8 ones

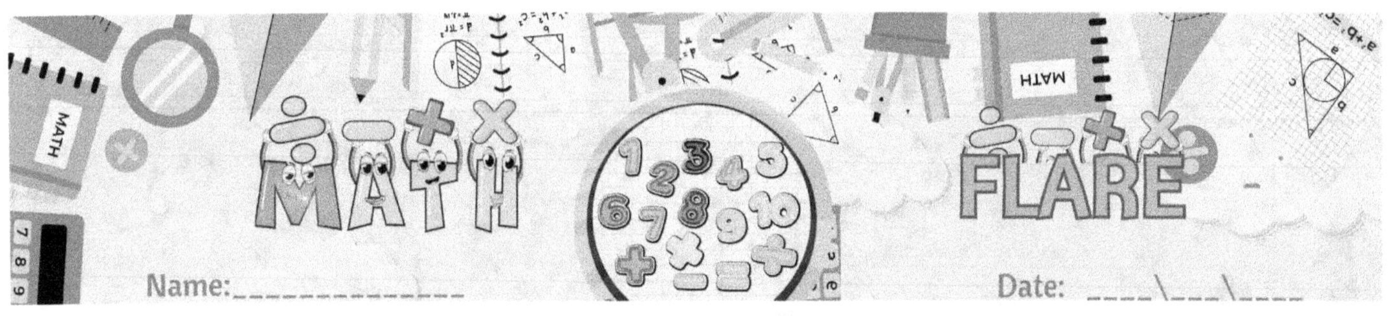

91) _________________ 2 ten thousands + 1 thousand + 3 hundreds + 1 ten + 1 one

92) _________________ 3 ten thousands + 9 thousands + 5 hundreds + 1 ten + 6 ones

93) _________________ 6 ten thousands + 3 thousands + 9 hundreds + 1 ten + 8 ones

94) _________________ 8 ten thousands + 9 thousands + 5 hundreds + 1 ten + 7 ones

95) _________________ 4 ten thousands + 2 hundreds + 1 ten

96) _________________ 2 ten thousands + 2 thousands + 2 hundreds + 1 ten + 8 ones

97) _________________ 5 ten thousands + 6 thousands + 1 hundred + 5 tens + 4 ones

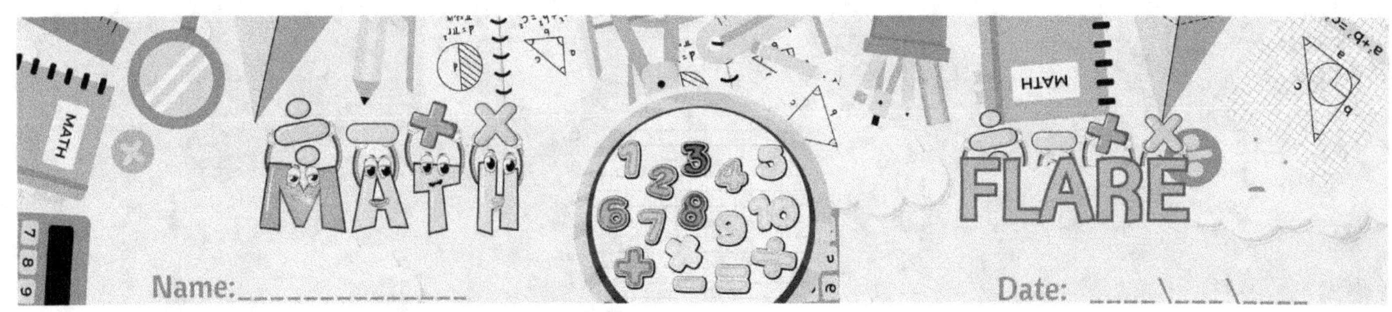

Place Value: Expanded Notation

Provide the expanded notation for each value.

1) 15,643   1 ten thousand + 5 thousands + 6 hundreds
              + 4 tens + 3 ones

2) 49,684

3) 39,980

4) 40,233

5) 35,055

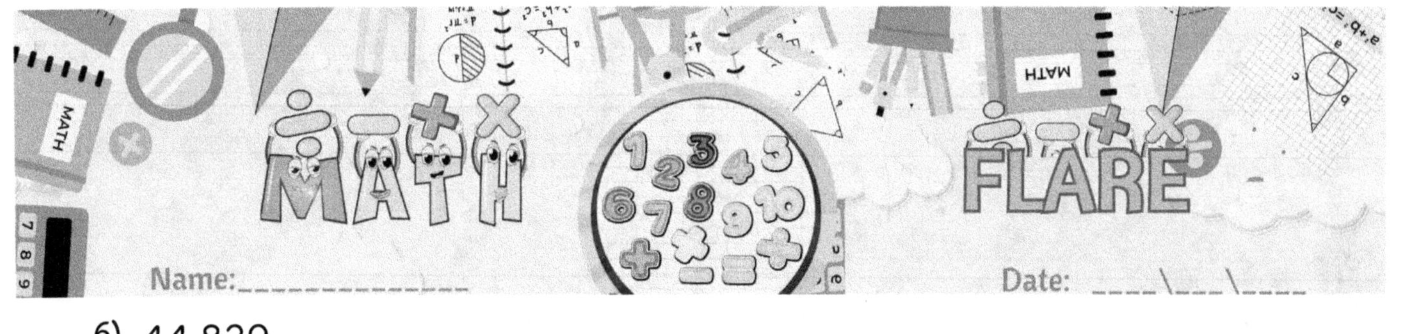

6) 44,829 ___________________________

7) 35,176 ___________________________

8) 31,050 ___________________________

9) 54,560 ___________________________

10) 63,686 ___________________________

11) 21,413 ___________________________

12) 31,573 ________________________
____

13) 90,106 ________________________
____

14) 93,944 ________________________
____

15) 12,093 ________________________
____

16) 55,912 ________________________
____

17) 39,591 ________________________
____

18) 47,124 ___________________________

19) 12,355 ___________________________

20) 85,798 ___________________________

21) 69,189 ___________________________

22) 70,936 ___________________________

23) 67,991 ___________________________

24) 22,911 ____

25) 93,477 ____

26) 91,395 ____

27) 71,803 ____

28) 82,516 ____

29) 93,486 ____

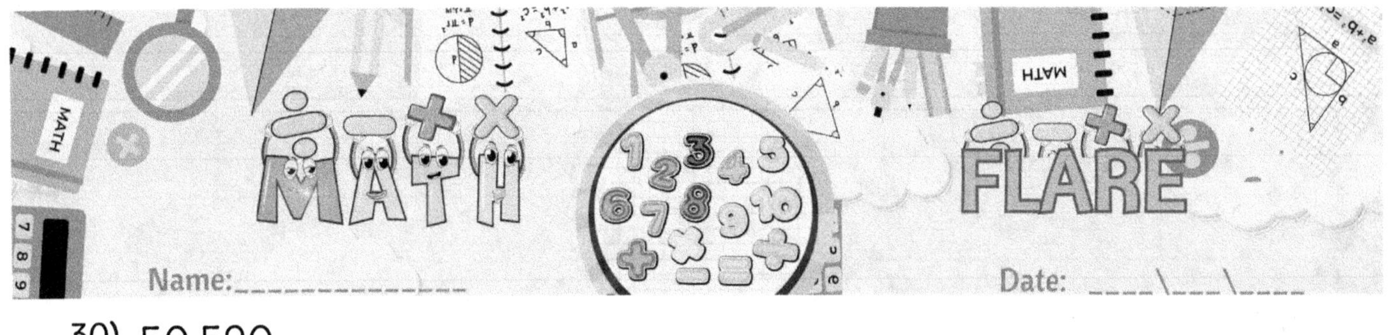

30) 50,590 _______________________________

____

31) 89,061 _______________________________

____

32) 60,430 _______________________________

____

33) 33,953 _______________________________

____

34) 21,512 _______________________________

____

35) 99,318 _______________________________

____

36) 74,522 ______________________

37) 13,916 ______________________

38) 17,804 ______________________

39) 92,483 ______________________

40) 36,377 ______________________

41) 51,301 ______________________

42) 74,826 _______________________________
____

43) 38,687 _______________________________
____

44) 38,269 _______________________________
____

45) 31,257 _______________________________
____

46) 38,741 _______________________________
____

47) 28,513 _______________________________
____

48) 84,463 ___________________________

49) 19,217 ___________________________

50) 83,603 ___________________________

51) 34,328 ___________________________

52) 52,392 ___________________________

53) 37,855 ___________________________

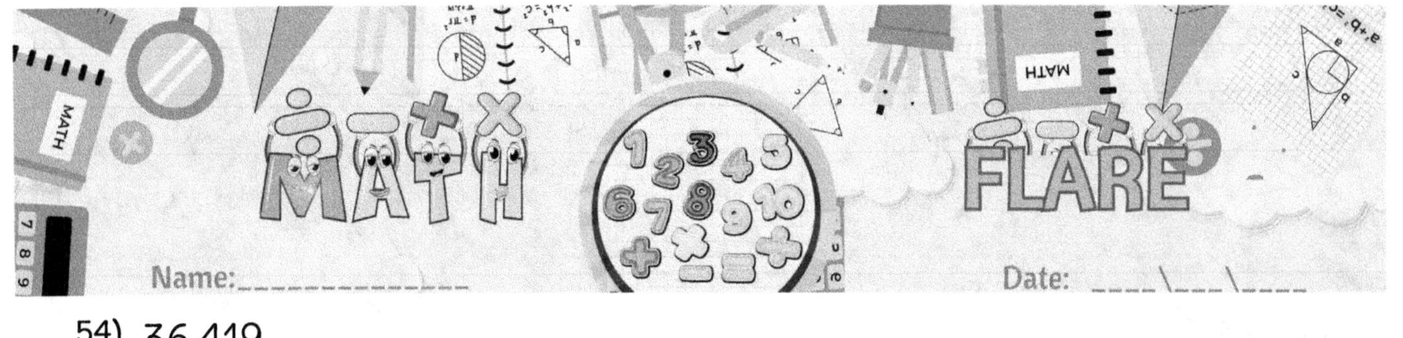

54) 36,419 ___________________

55) 86,964 ___________________

56) 44,706 ___________________

57) 81,693 ___________________

58) 27,069 ___________________

59) 46,755 ___________________

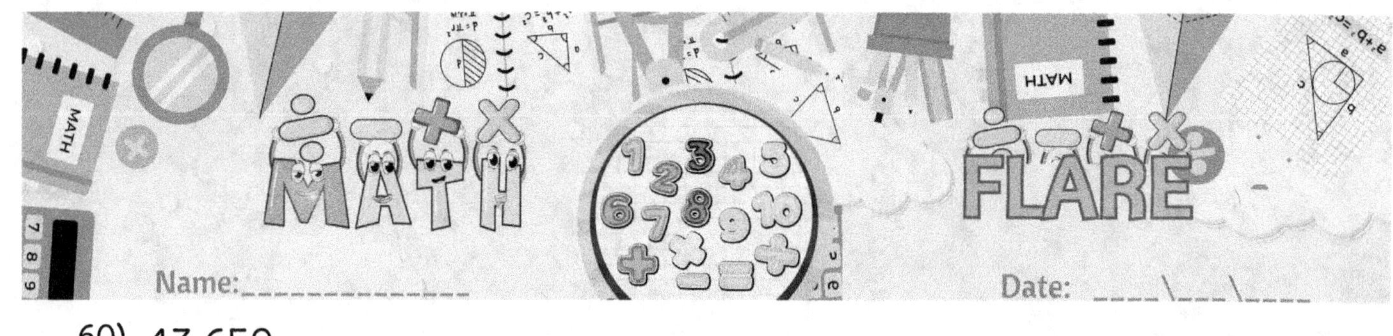

60) 43,659 _______________________
____

61) 73,025 _______________________
____

62) 52,659 _______________________
____

63) 37,562 _______________________
____

64) 13,970 _______________________
____

65) 74,625 _______________________
____

66) 60,982 __________________________

67) 97,618 __________________________

68) 78,594 __________________________

69) 94,625 __________________________

70) 37,571 __________________________

71) 51,995 __________________________

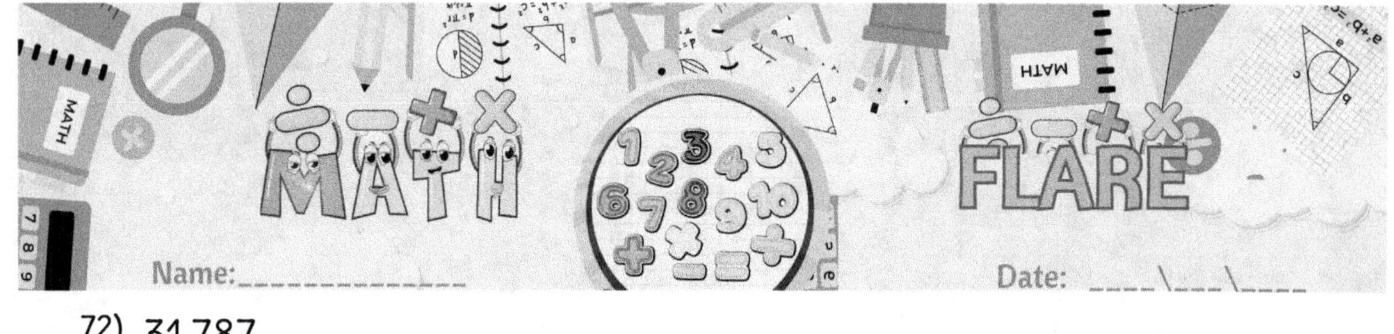

72) 31,787 _______________________

____

73) 54,640 _______________________

____

74) 75,977 _______________________

____

75) 44,497 _______________________

____

76) 94,363 _______________________

____

77) 42,249 _______________________

____

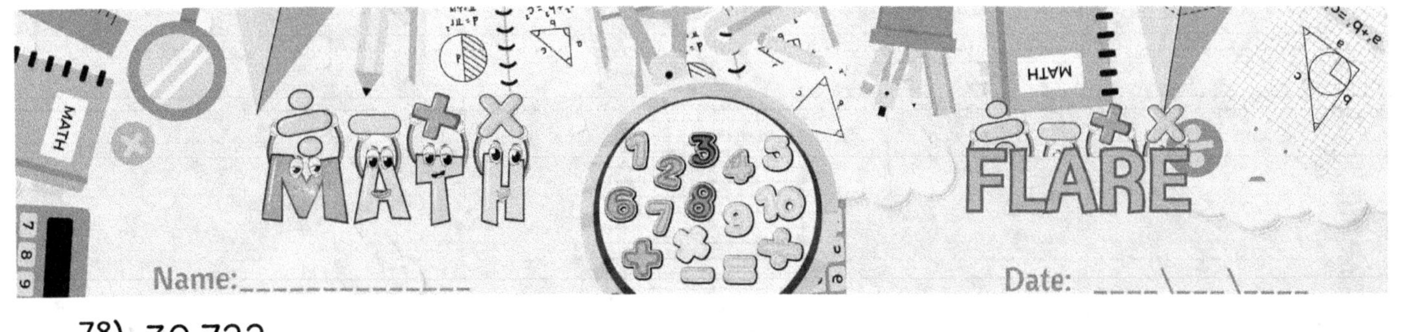

78) 39,722 _______________________________

79) 91,653 _______________________________

80) 64,735 _______________________________

81) 72,882 _______________________________

82) 87,339 _______________________________

83) 73,299 _______________________________

84) 19,883   __________________________
____

85) 26,263   __________________________
____

86) 46,668   __________________________
____

87) 32,576   __________________________
____

88) 97,533   __________________________
____

89) 34,547   __________________________
____

Place Value: Expanded Notation

Provide the expanded notation for each value.

1) ___64,612___   60,000 + 4,000 + 600 + 10 + 2

2) ________________   90,000 + 2,000 + 800 + 20 + 8

3) ________________   80,000 + 6,000 + 800 + 40 + 7

4) ________________   70,000 + 1,000 + 40 + 7

5) ________________   50,000 + 8,000 + 800 + 20 + 4

6) ________________   60,000 + 3,000 + 300 + 50

7) ________________   90,000 + 8,000 + 600 + 40 + 1

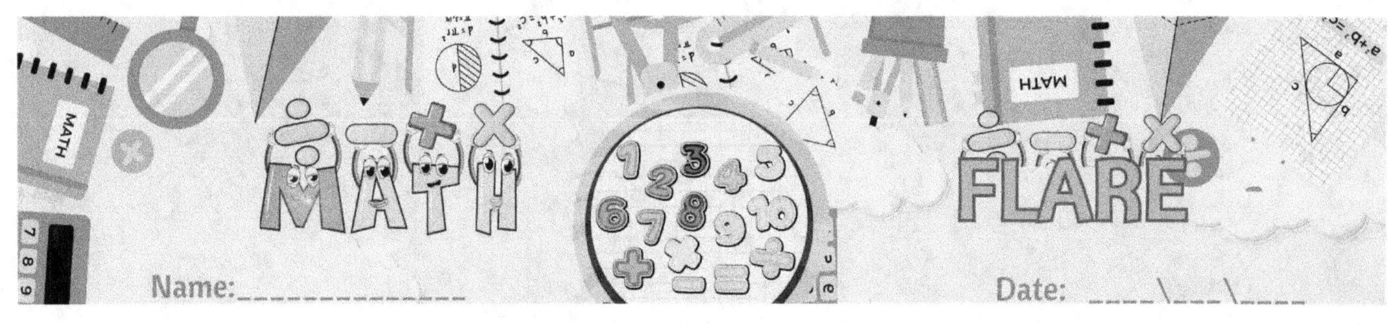

8) _______________________ 40,000 + 7,000 + 200 + 60 + 3

9) _______________________ 30,000 + 4,000 + 700 + 10 + 7

10) _______________________ 60,000 + 3,000 + 600 + 40 + 3

11) _______________________ 70,000 + 200 + 70 + 4

12) _______________________ 40,000 + 1,000 + 100 + 20 + 2

13) _______________________ 40,000 + 9,000 + 900 + 10 + 8

14) _______________________ 80,000 + 9,000 + 800 + 30 + 7

15) _______________________ 80,000 + 1,000 + 600 + 40 + 6

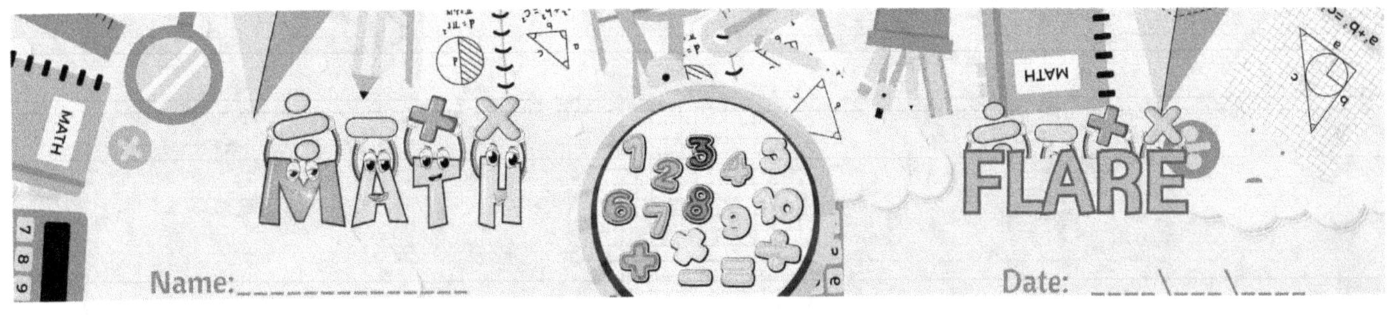

16) _________________   40,000 + 1,000 + 600 + 8

17) _________________   10,000 + 2,000 + 500 + 40

18) _________________   90,000 + 7,000 + 700 + 50 + 1

19) _________________   60,000 + 1,000 + 800 + 70 + 7

20) _________________   90,000 + 1,000 + 900 + 20 + 1

21) _________________   90,000 + 2,000 + 600

22) _________________   10,000 + 2,000 + 400 + 50 + 8

23) _________________   50,000 + 1,000 + 900 + 70 + 1

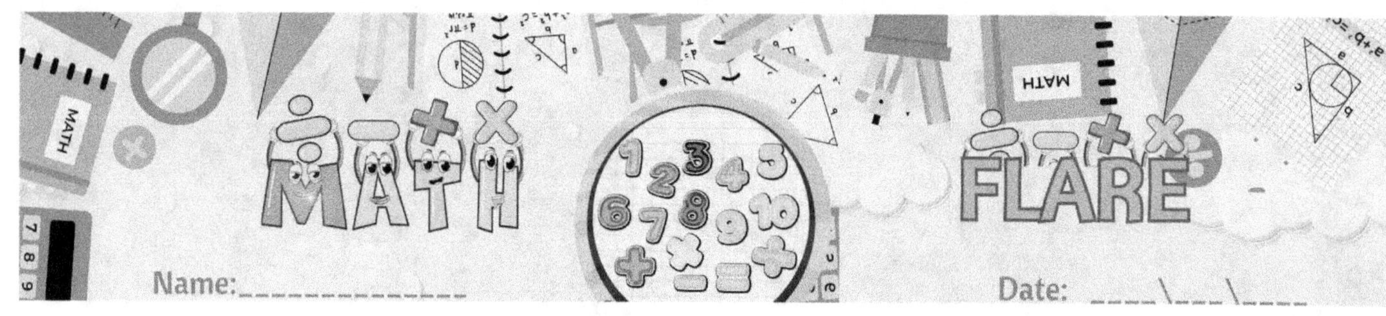

24) _________________ 30,000 + 5,000 + 400 + 10 + 4

25) _________________ 80,000 + 2,000 + 10 + 9

26) _________________ 70,000 + 700 + 70 + 5

27) _________________ 80,000 + 5,000 + 600 + 80 + 5

28) _________________ 70,000 + 9,000 + 300 + 50 + 9

29) _________________ 20,000 + 7,000 + 600 + 80

30) _________________ 80,000 + 7,000 + 700 + 6

31) _________________ 30,000 + 7,000 + 900 + 50 + 6

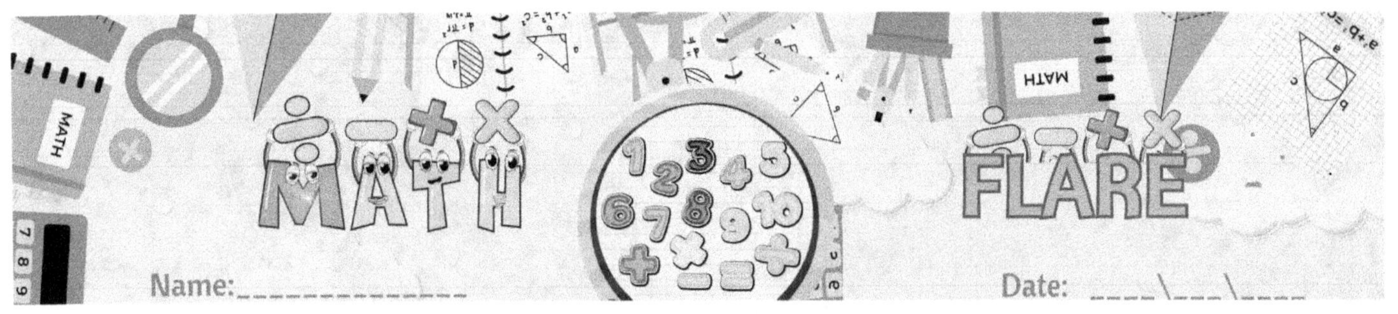

32) _________________ 30,000 + 8,000 + 400 + 6

33) _________________ 10,000 + 80 + 5

34) _________________ 50,000 + 4,000 + 40 + 6

35) _________________ 40,000 + 10 + 3

36) _________________ 40,000 + 4,000 + 700 + 40 + 1

37) _________________ 60,000 + 5,000 + 100 + 40 + 8

38) _________________ 60,000 + 700 + 30 + 9

39) _________________ 90,000 + 5,000 + 800 + 10 + 5

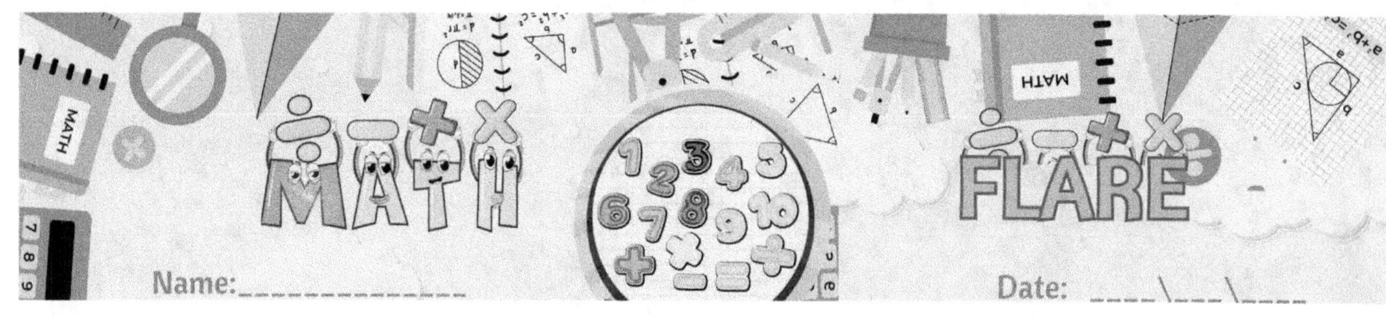

40) _________________ 20,000 + 2,000 + 600 + 20 + 7

41) _________________ 40,000 + 5,000 + 800 + 50 + 5

42) _________________ 50,000 + 7,000 + 100

43) _________________ 10,000 + 7,000 + 500 + 30 + 1

44) _________________ 70,000 + 6,000 + 70 + 8

45) _________________ 30,000 + 1,000 + 300 + 70 + 9

46) _________________ 30,000 + 3,000 + 600 + 10 + 3

47) _________________ 30,000 + 2,000 + 900 + 60 + 4

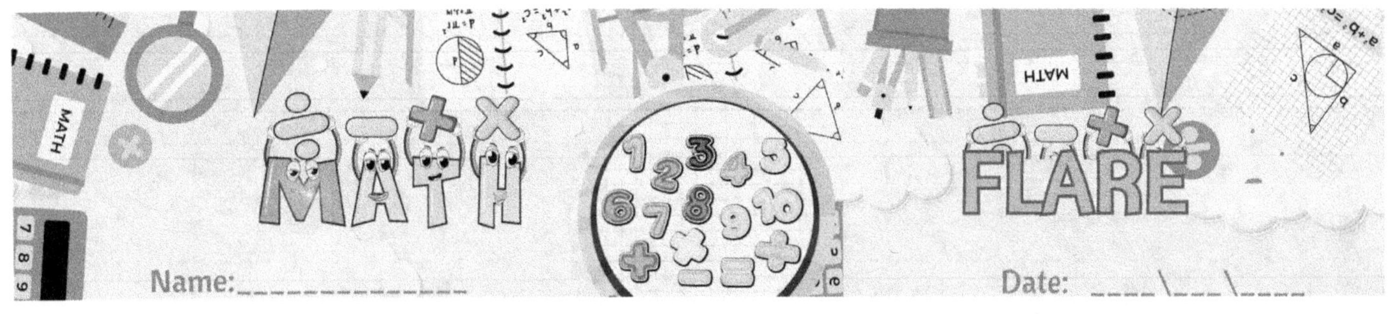

48) _______________ 90,000 + 7,000 + 500 + 2

49) _______________ 90,000 + 1,000 + 600 + 50 + 2

50) _______________ 70,000 + 8,000 + 200 + 70 + 4

51) _______________ 20,000 + 3,000 + 700 + 20 + 2

52) _______________ 40,000 + 8,000 + 900 + 10 + 6

53) _______________ 70,000 + 600 + 90 + 8

54) _______________ 10,000 + 5,000 + 600 + 10 + 2

55) _______________ 40,000 + 1,000 + 900 + 40 + 7

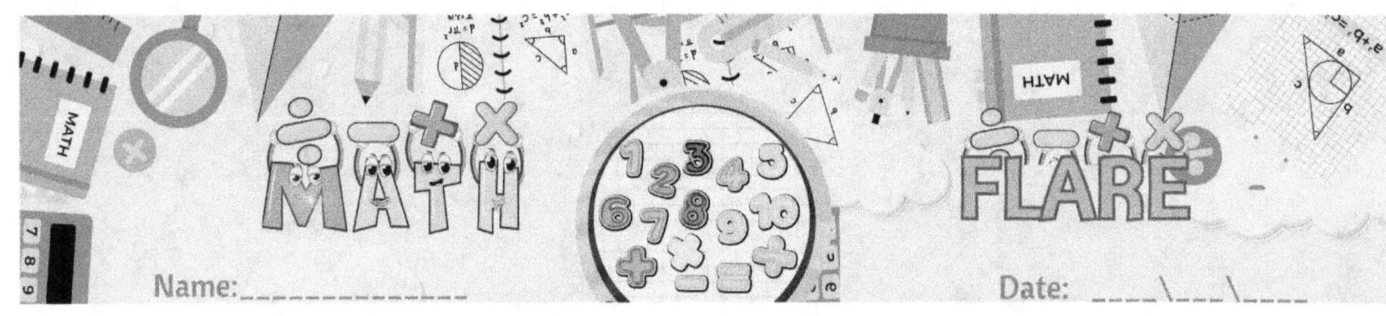

56) _________________ 60,000 + 2,000 + 100 + 50 + 4

57) _________________ 50,000 + 800 + 50 + 8

58) _________________ 60,000 + 1,000 + 400 + 30 + 3

59) _________________ 80,000 + 9,000 + 20 + 7

60) _________________ 80,000 + 8,000 + 40 + 8

61) _________________ 70,000 + 7,000 + 600 + 60 + 5

62) _________________ 20,000 + 9,000 + 200 + 80 + 1

63) _________________ 20,000 + 9,000 + 500 + 80 + 3

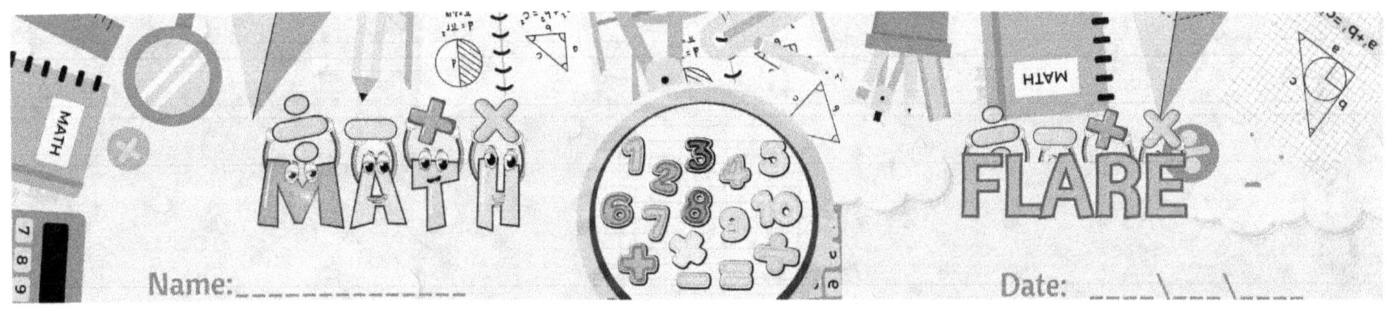

64) _________________ 40,000 + 7,000 + 10

65) _________________ 30,000 + 5,000 + 600 + 80 + 7

66) _________________ 40,000 + 1,000 + 800 + 60 + 8

67) _________________ 40,000 + 1,000 + 30 + 7

68) _________________ 90,000 + 5,000 + 800 + 70 + 1

69) _________________ 50,000 + 9,000 + 800 + 20 + 4

70) _________________ 40,000 + 6,000 + 900 + 5

71) _________________ 70,000 + 6,000 + 400 + 60

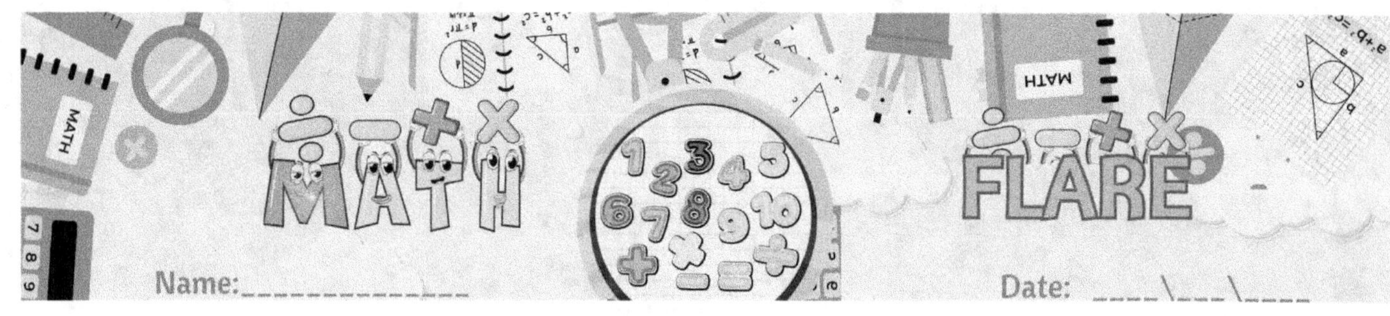

72) _______________ 50,000 + 1,000 + 800 + 1

73) _______________ 10,000 + 1,000 + 900 + 30 + 6

74) _______________ 40,000 + 9,000 + 200 + 50

75) _______________ 50,000 + 6,000 + 60 + 6

76) _______________ 40,000 + 5,000 + 500

77) _______________ 90,000 + 4,000 + 900 + 20 + 5

78) _______________ 70,000 + 5,000 + 800 + 90 + 2

79) _______________ 10,000 + 4,000 + 30 + 5

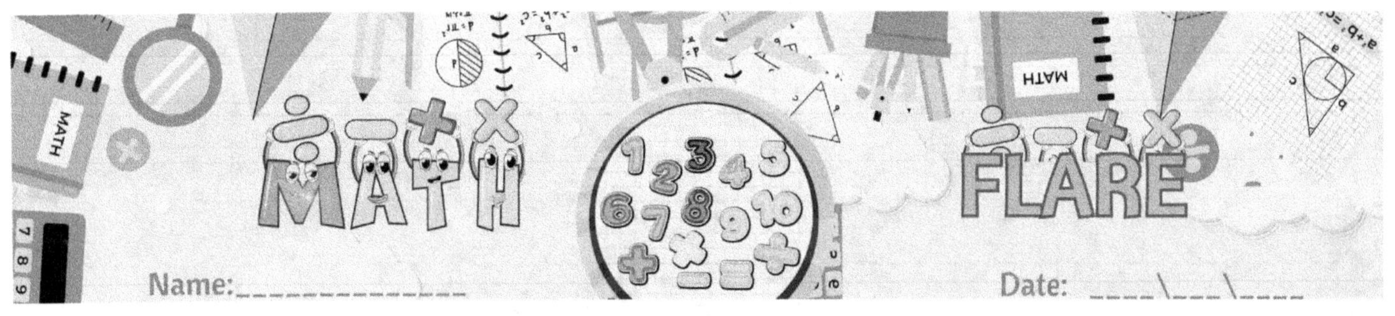

80) _________________ 50,000 + 8,000 + 400 + 6

81) _________________ 40,000 + 7,000 + 800 + 10 + 1

82) _________________ 80,000 + 8,000 + 100 + 80 + 2

83) _________________ 40,000 + 9,000 + 400 + 5

84) _________________ 70,000 + 3,000 + 900 + 80 + 4

85) _________________ 80,000 + 9,000 + 40

86) _________________ 60,000 + 7,000 + 700 + 7

87) _________________ 90,000 + 4,000 + 400 + 70 + 2

Understanding Time

Draw clock hands to show the passage of time.

1) 

What time will it be in 3 hours 8 minutes 14 seconds?

2) 

What time will it be in 9 hours 20 minutes 46 seconds?

3) 

What time was it 8 hours 50 minutes 1 second ago?

4) 

What time will it be in 10 hours 8 minutes 43 seconds?

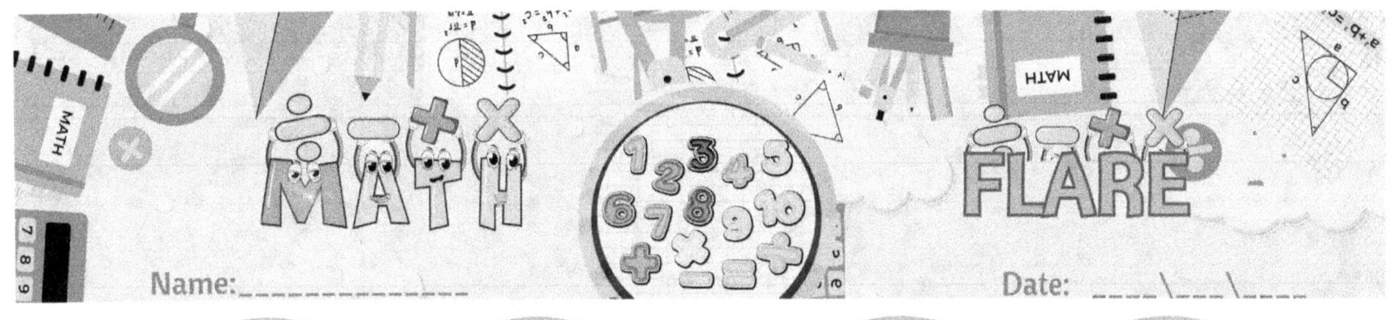

5)

What time will it be in 9 hours 56 minutes 41 seconds?

6)

What time will it be in 7 hours 13 minutes 18 seconds?

7)

What time was it 10 hours 24 minutes 3 seconds ago?

8)

What time will it be in 5 hours 29 minutes 29 seconds?

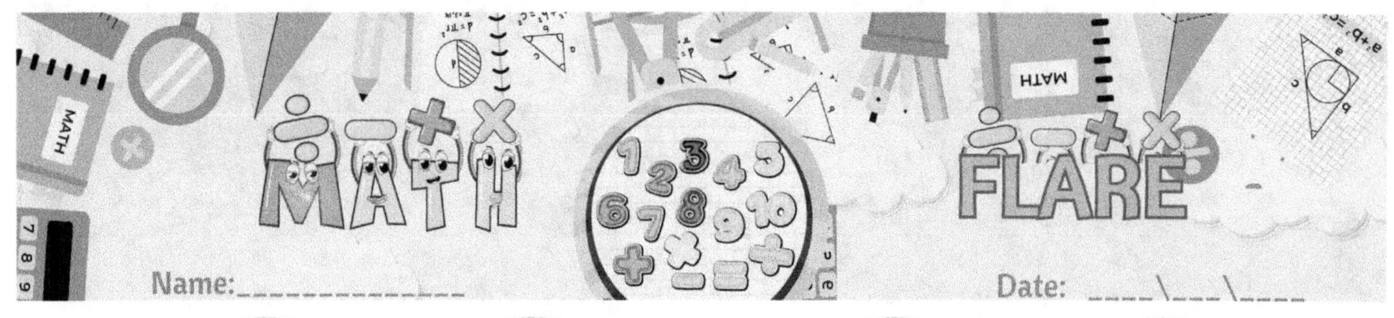

9)

What time will it be in 11 hours 22 minutes 0 seconds?

10)

What time was it 9 hours 1 minute 24 seconds ago?

11)

What time will it be in 5 hours 2 minutes 37 seconds?

12)

What time will it be in 2 hours 2 minutes 44 seconds?

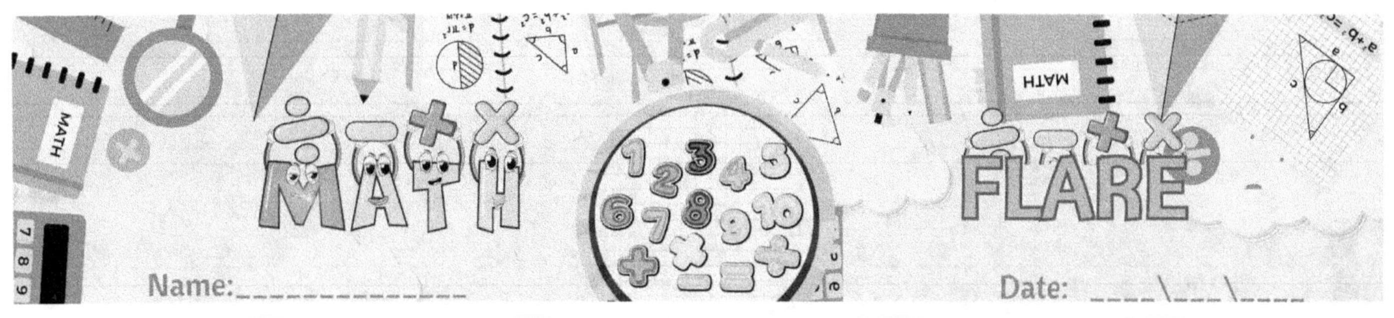

13)

What time was it 1 hour 16 minutes 27 seconds ago?

14)

What time was it 2 hours 35 minutes 50 seconds ago?

15)

What time will it be in 1 hour 5 minutes 22 seconds?

16)

What time will it be in 2 hours 1 minute 26 seconds?

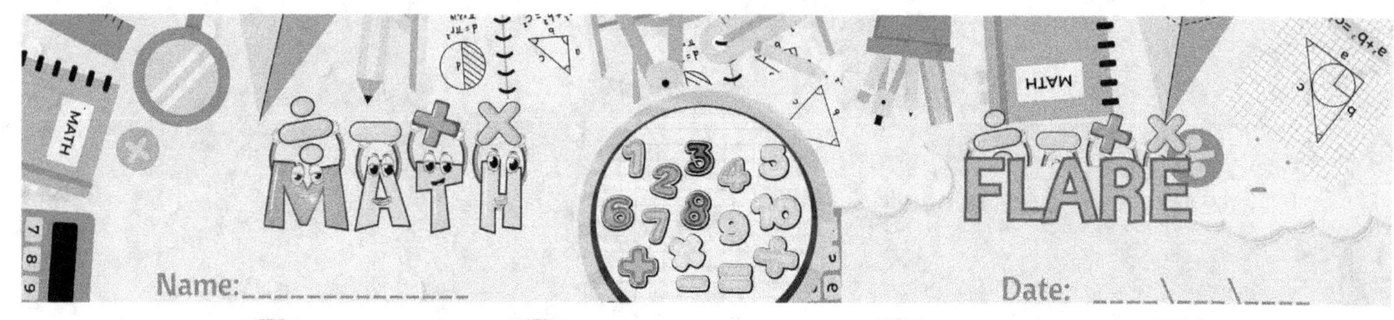

17)

What time will it be in 2 hours 52 minutes 20 seconds?

18)

What time will it be in 4 hours 45 minutes 44 seconds?

19)

What time was it 5 hours 17 minutes 26 seconds ago?

20)

What time will it be in 11 hours 4 minutes 56 seconds?

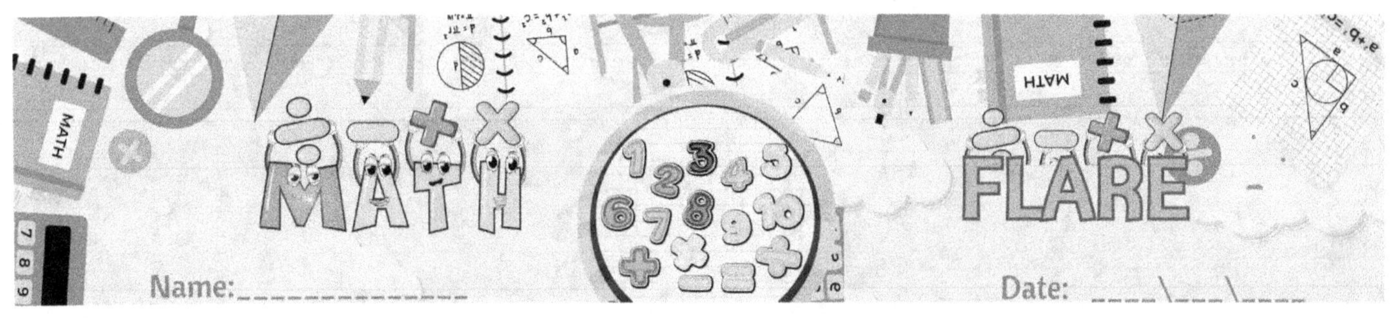

21) What time was it 2 hours 51 minutes 15 seconds ago?

22) What time will it be in 6 hours 59 minutes 43 seconds?

23) What time will it be in 2 hours 42 minutes 20 seconds?

24) What time was it 10 hours 43 minutes 44 seconds ago?

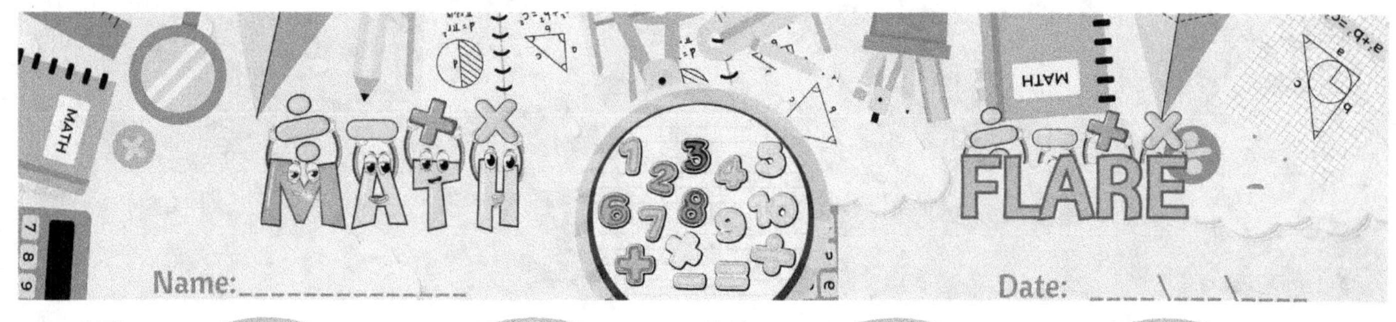

25) 

What time will it be in 11 hours 12 minutes 48 seconds?

26) 

What time will it be in 6 hours 11 minutes 53 seconds?

27) 

What time was it 4 hours 53 minutes 17 seconds ago?

28) 

What time was it 3 hours 49 minutes 21 seconds ago?

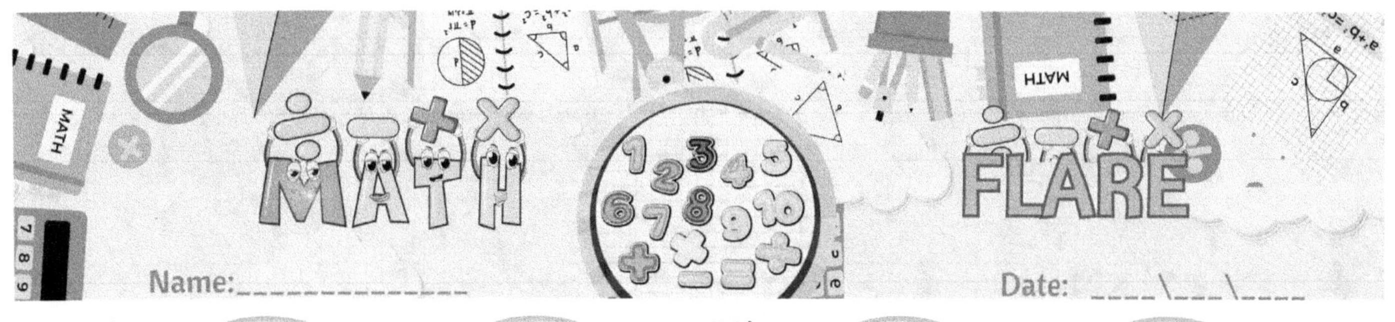

29) 

What time was it 7 hours 16 minutes 8 seconds ago?

30) 

What time will it be in 10 hours 33 minutes 47 seconds?

31) 

What time will it be in 1 hour 35 minutes 30 seconds?

32) 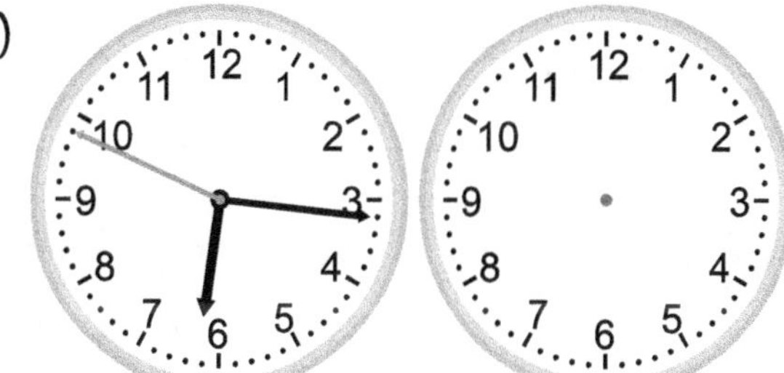

What time was it 1 hour 33 minutes 49 seconds ago?

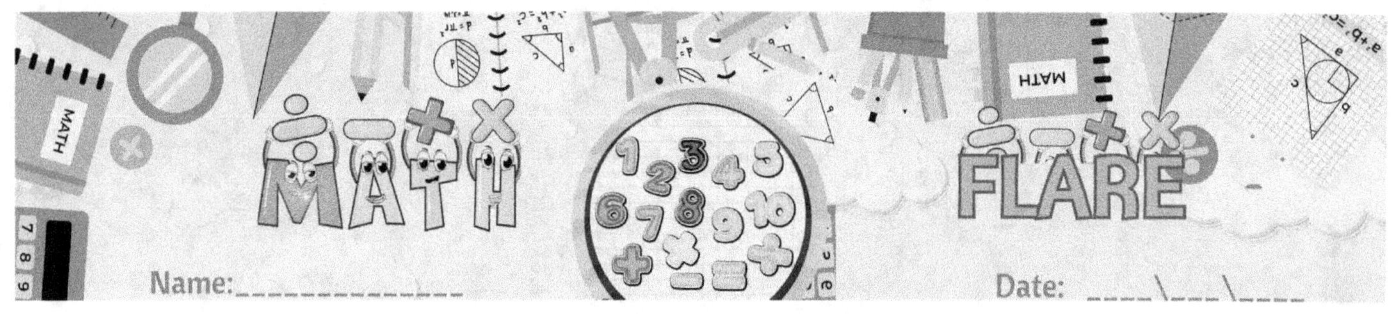

33)

What time will it be in 8 hours 42 minutes 22 seconds?

34)

What time will it be in 4 hours 53 minutes 55 seconds?

35)

What time was it 5 hours 25 minutes 19 seconds ago?

36)

What time will it be in 3 hours 13 minutes 14 seconds?

37)

What time was it 3 hours 32 minutes 42 seconds ago?

38)

What time was it 3 hours 12 minutes 51 seconds ago?

39)

What time was it 3 hours 44 minutes 41 seconds ago?

40)

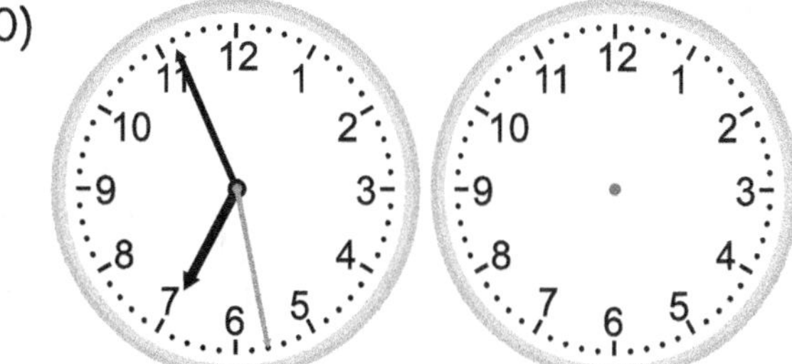

What time was it 11 hours 41 minutes 8 seconds ago?

Chapter. 04

Geometry

Area and Perimeter

The area of a shape represents the amount of space it occupies. The perimeter of a shape is the total distance around its outer edge.

Area of Rectangle

For a square, since all four sides are equal, we only need to know the length of one side to find its area. We can calculate the area of a square by multiplying the length of one side by itself (squared). So, if the length of one side of the square is 's', then the area (A) is given by:

$$A = s \times s$$

4 in

4 in

$$A = 4 \times 4$$
$$A = 16$$

Perimeter of Rectangle

For a square, since all four sides are equal, we can find the perimeter by adding up the lengths of all four sides. If 's' represents the length of one side, then the perimeter (P) is given by:

$$P = 4 \times s$$

$$P = 4 \times 4$$

$$P = 16$$

Area of Triangle:

The area of a triangle represents the amount of space enclosed within its three sides. The formula for calculating the area of a triangle depends on the type of triangle. For a general triangle, we use the formula:

$$A = \frac{1}{2} \times base \times height$$

Where:

- *A* represents the area of the triangle.

- The base is the length of any one side of the triangle.

- The height is the perpendicular distance from the base to the opposite vertex.

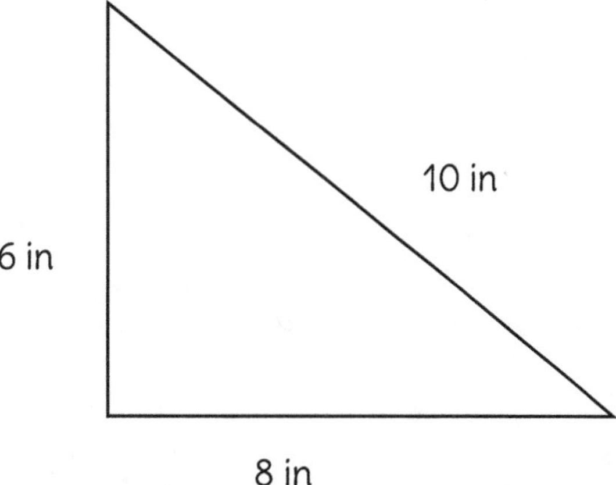

$$A = \frac{1}{2} \times \text{base} \times \text{height}$$

$$A = \frac{1}{2} \times 6 \times 8$$

$$A = \frac{1}{2} \times 48$$

$$A = 24$$

Perimeter of Triangle:

The perimeter of a triangle is the total length of its three sides. To find the perimeter, we simply add the lengths of all three sides together:

$$P = side1 + side2 + side3$$

$$P = 6 + 8 + 10$$

$$P = 24$$

Area and Perimeter: Rectangles and Triangles

1)

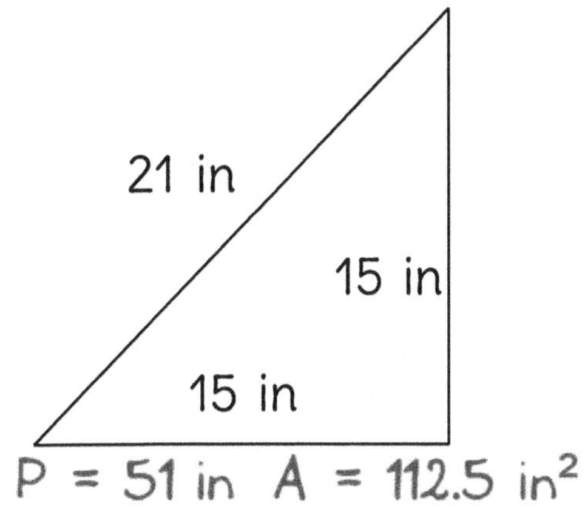

P = 51 in   A = 112.5 in²

2)

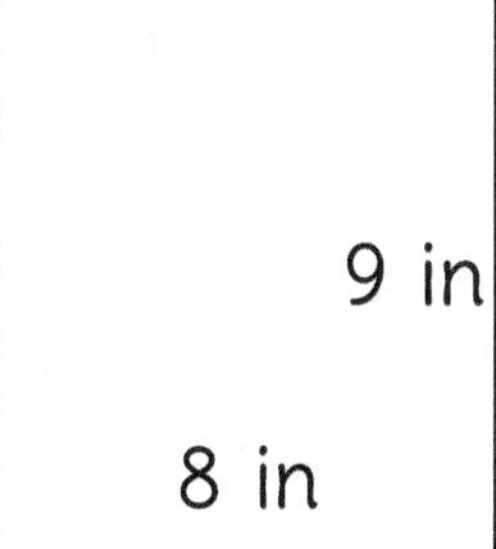

3)

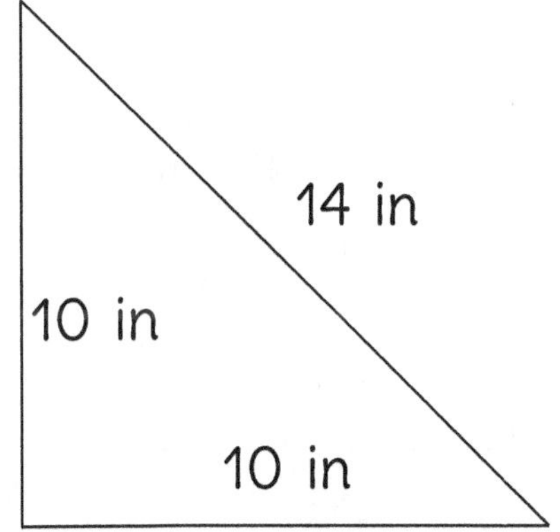

4)

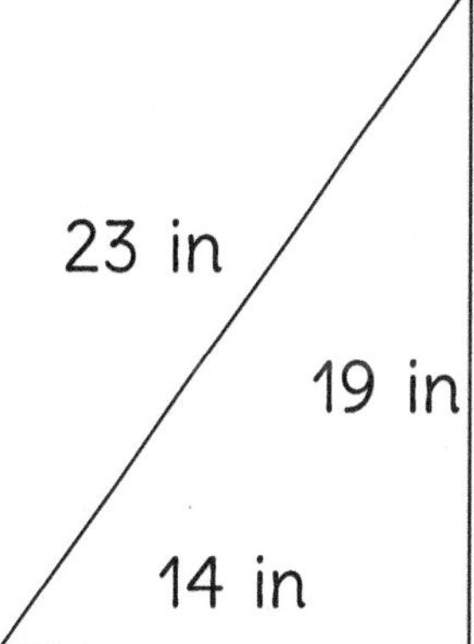

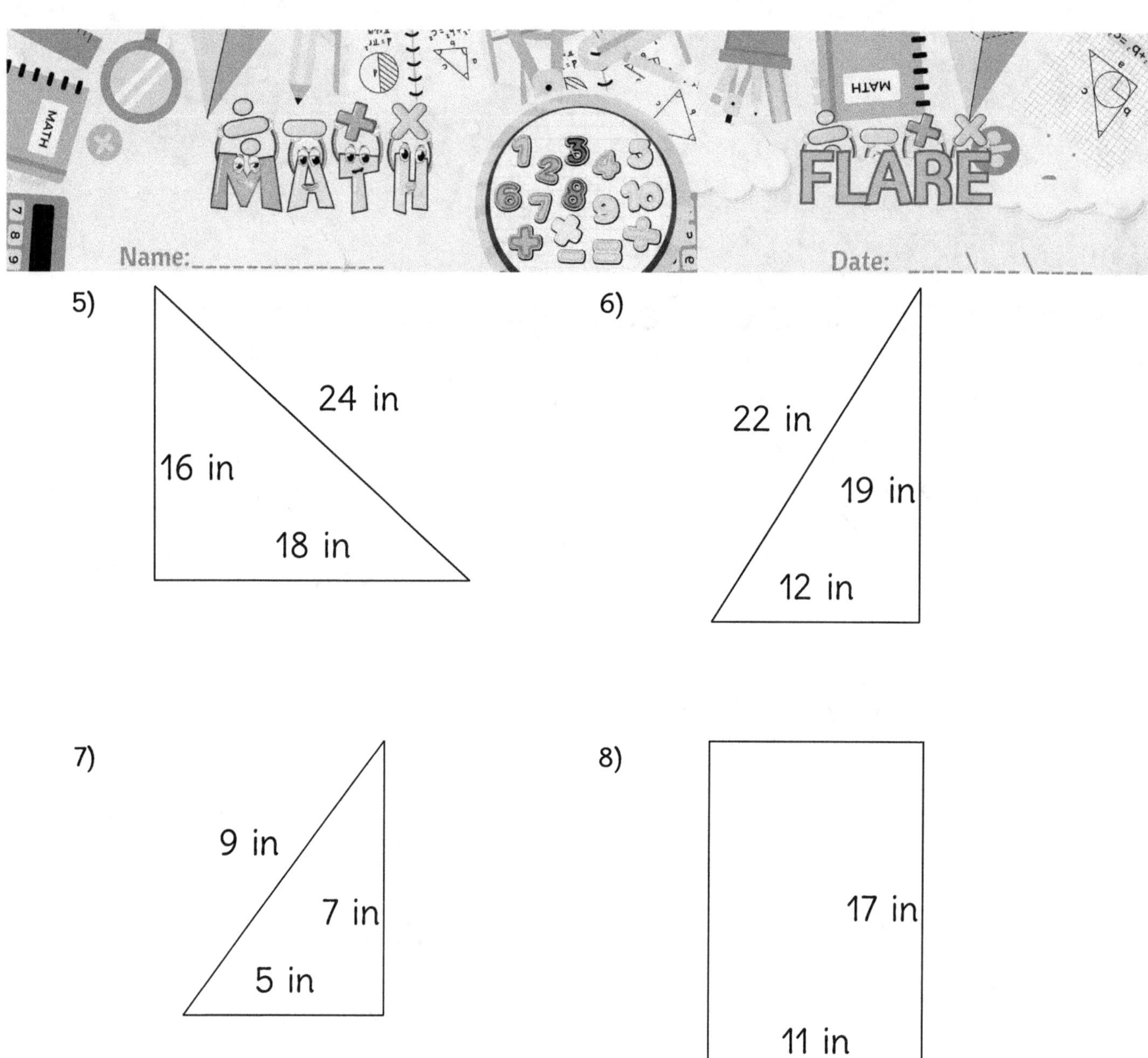
Name:
Date:
MATH
FLARE

5)
24 in
16 in
18 in

6)
22 in
19 in
12 in

7)
9 in
7 in
5 in

8)
17 in
11 in

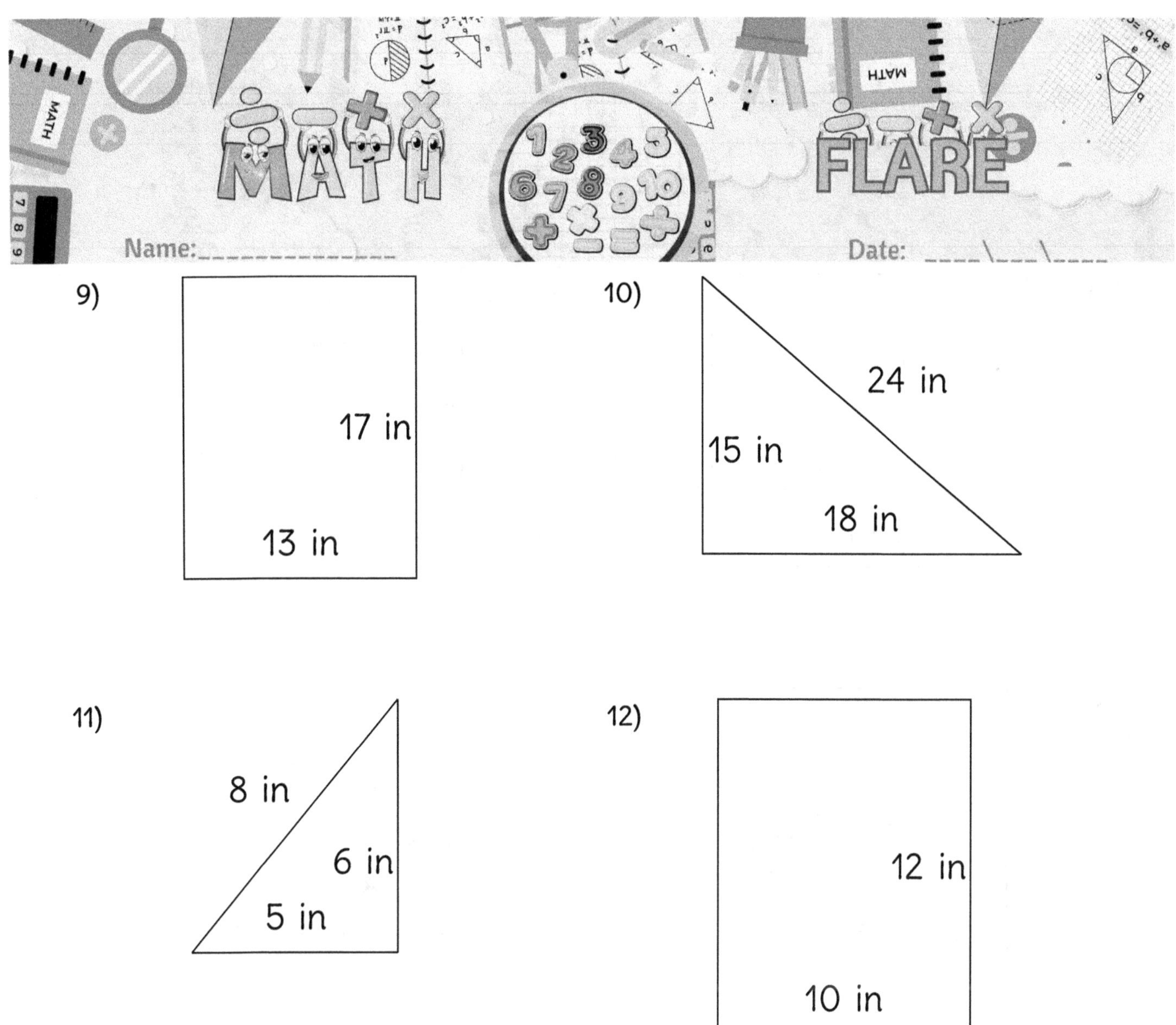
9)
17 in
13 in
10)
24 in
15 in
18 in
11)
8 in
6 in
5 in
12)
12 in
10 in

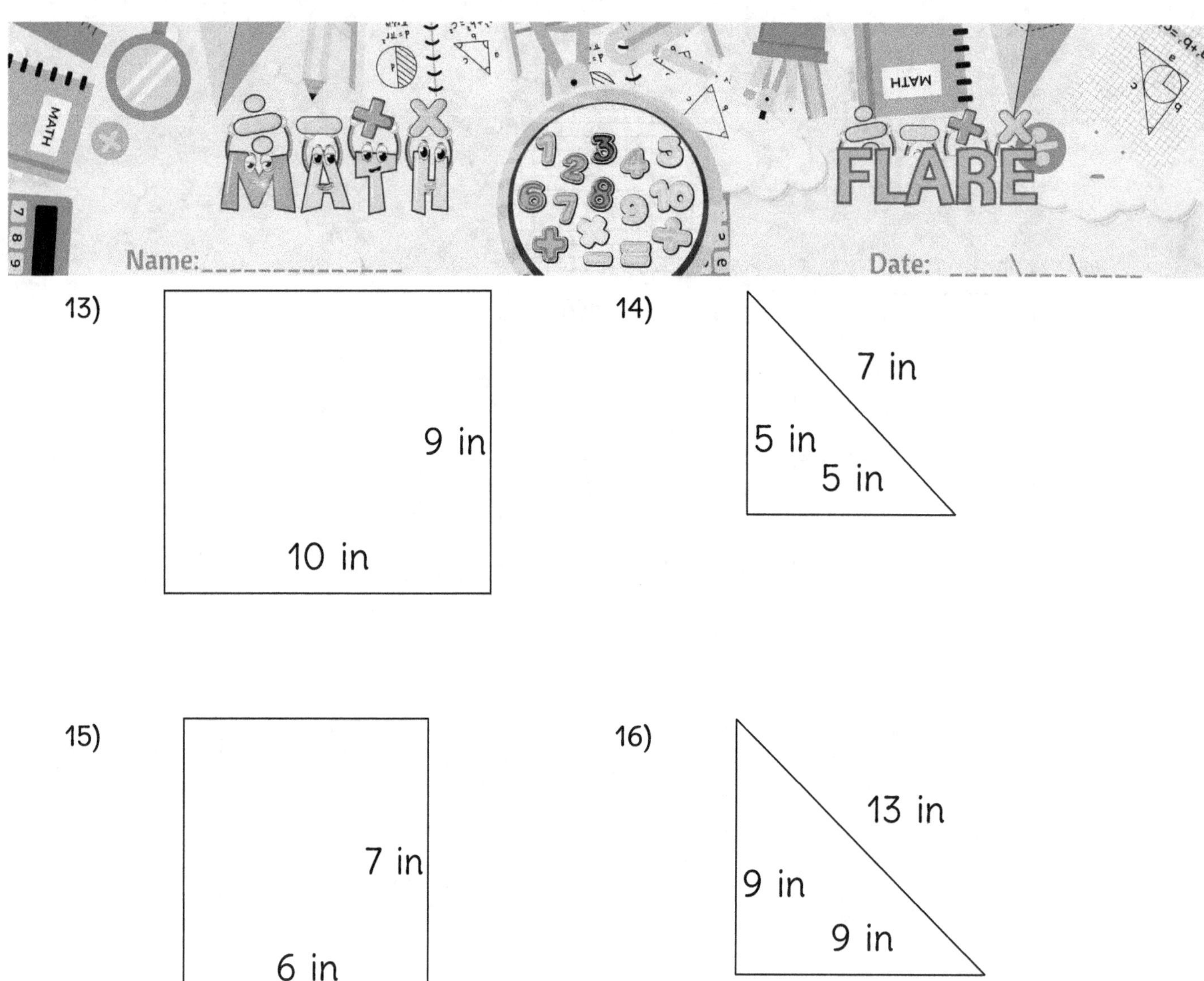

Name:
Date:
13)
9 in
10 in
14)
7 in
5 in
5 in
15)
7 in
6 in
16)
13 in
9 in
9 in

MATH FLARE
Name:
Date:

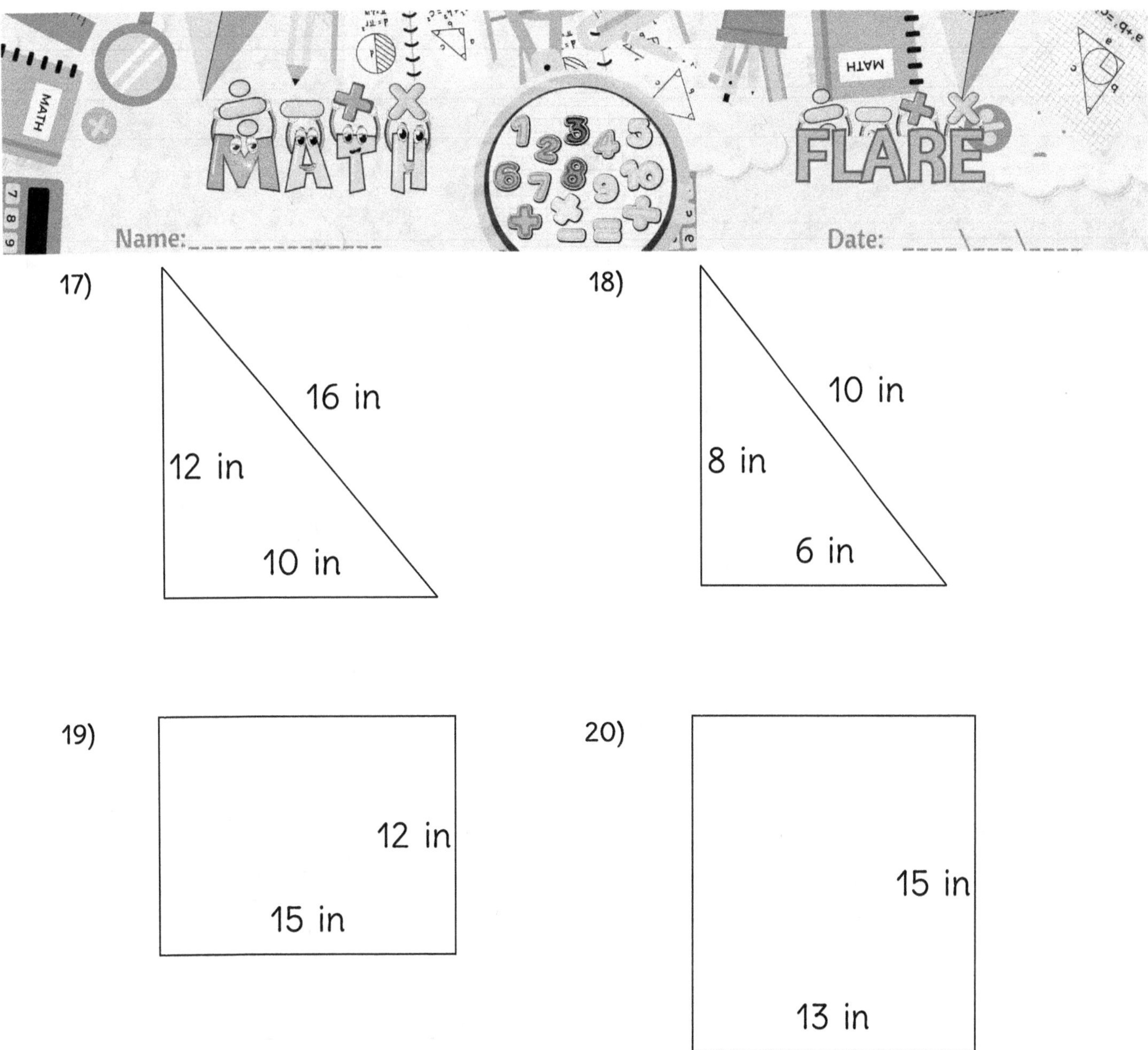

17)
16 in
12 in
10 in

18)
10 in
8 in
6 in

19)
12 in
15 in

20)
15 in
13 in

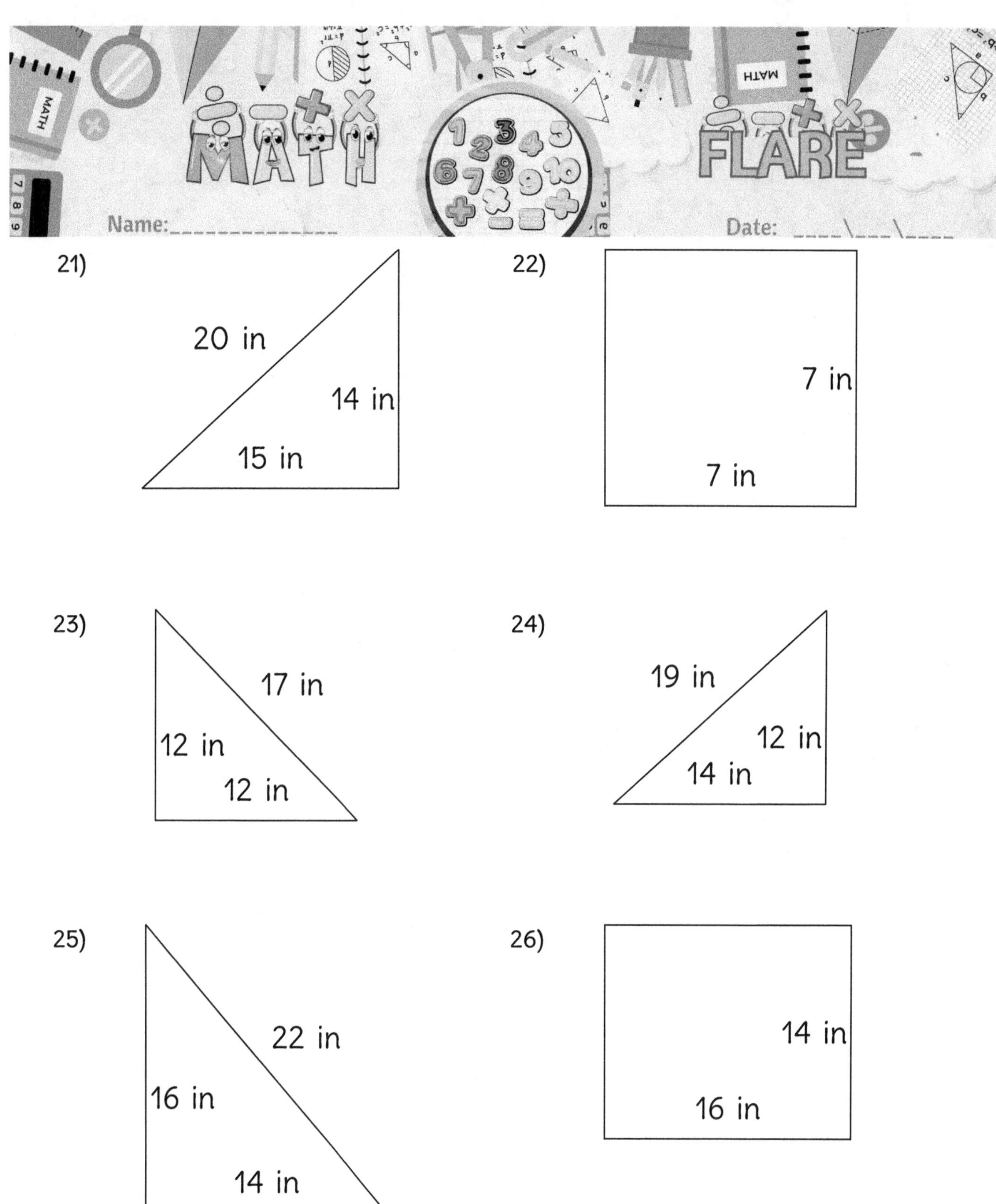
21)
20 in
14 in
15 in

22)
7 in
7 in

23)
17 in
12 in
12 in

24)
19 in
12 in
14 in

25)
22 in
16 in
14 in

26)
14 in
16 in

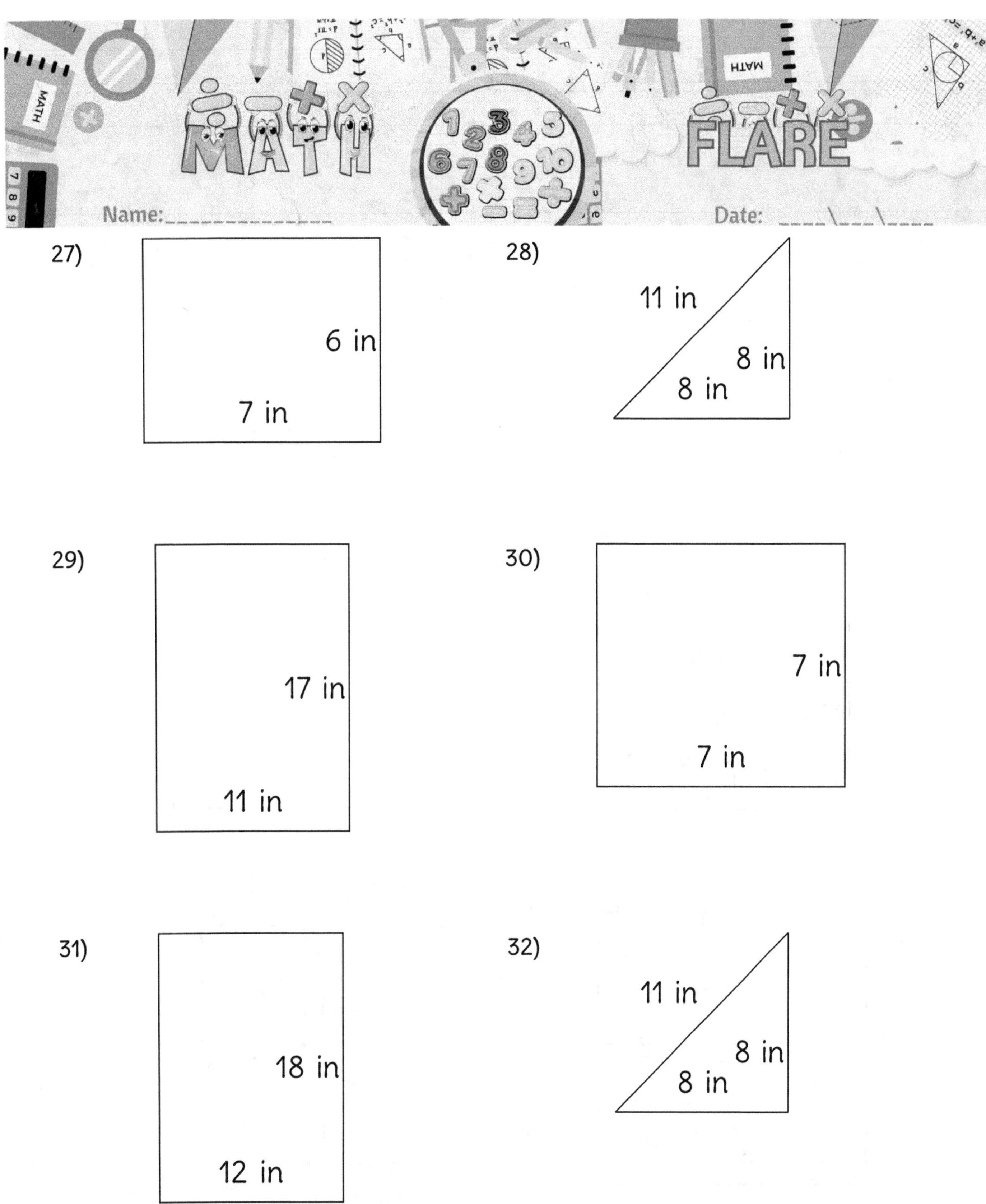
27)
6 in
7 in

28)
11 in
8 in
8 in

29)
17 in
11 in

30)
7 in
7 in

31)
18 in
12 in

32)
11 in
8 in
8 in

Name:
Date:

33)

10 in
6 in
8 in

34)
11 in
13 in

35)
14 in
11 in
9 in

36)
14 in
14 in

37)
8 in
8 in

38)
16 in
13 in
10 in

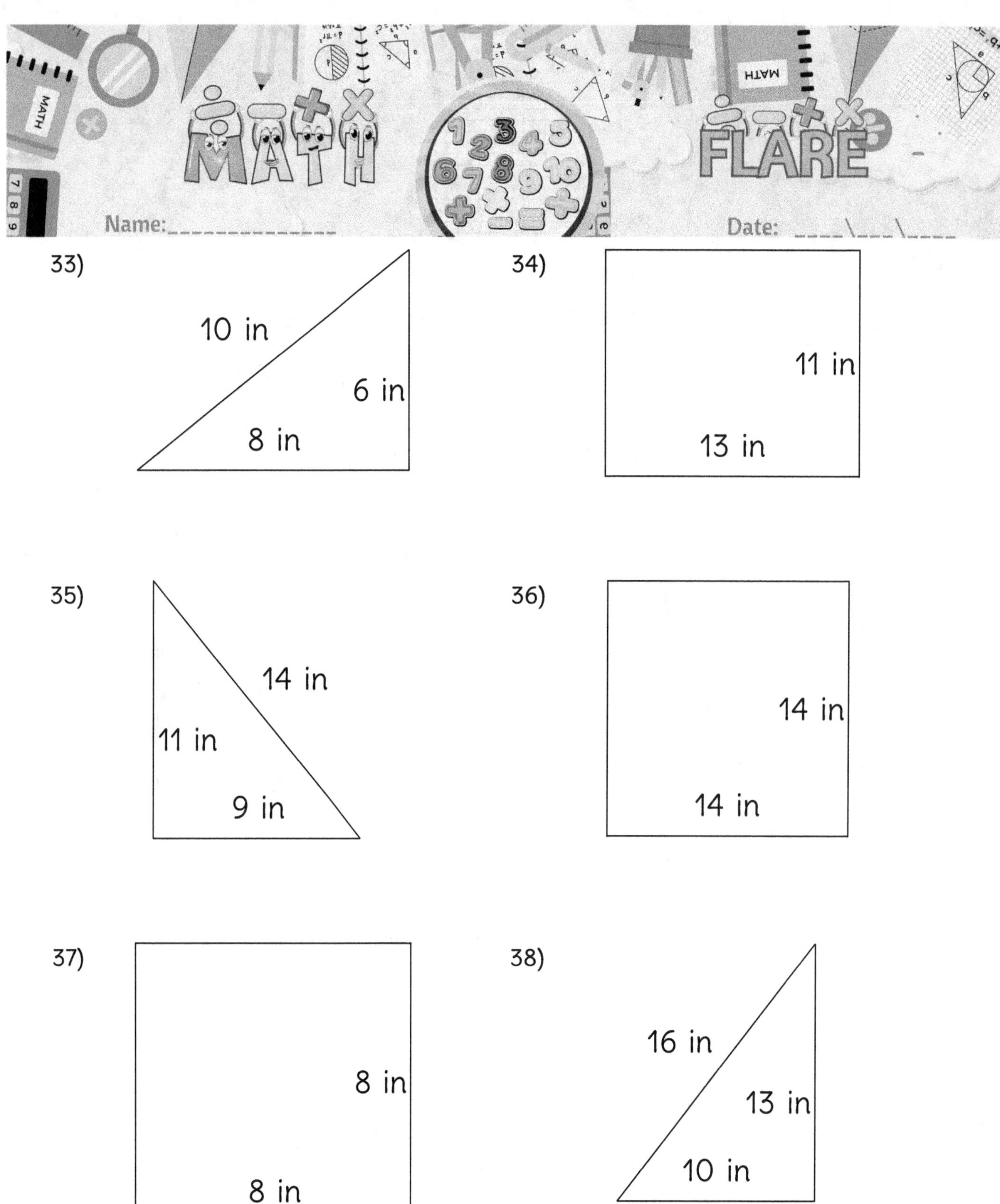

39)

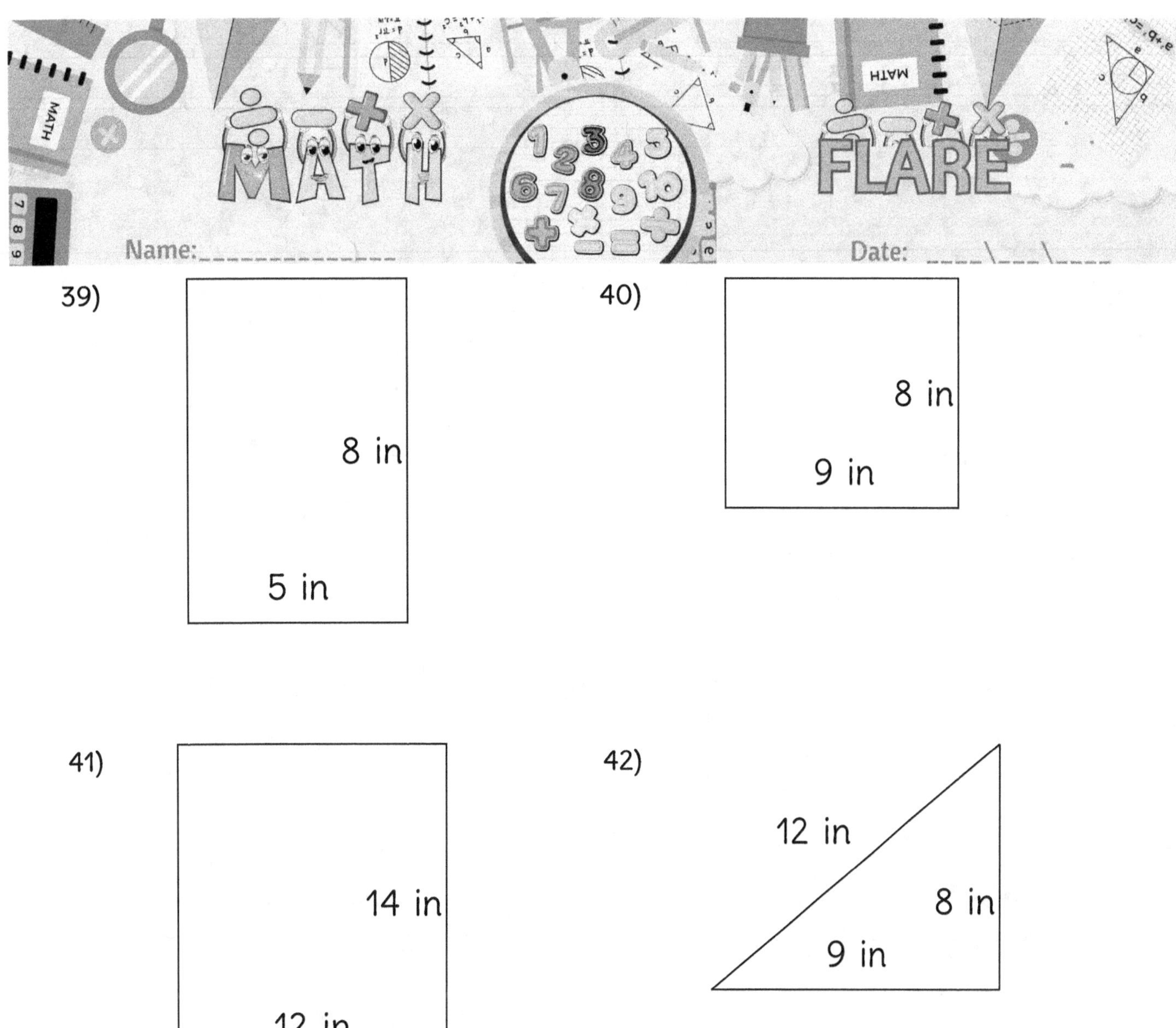

40)

41)

42)

Name:______________
Date: ____________

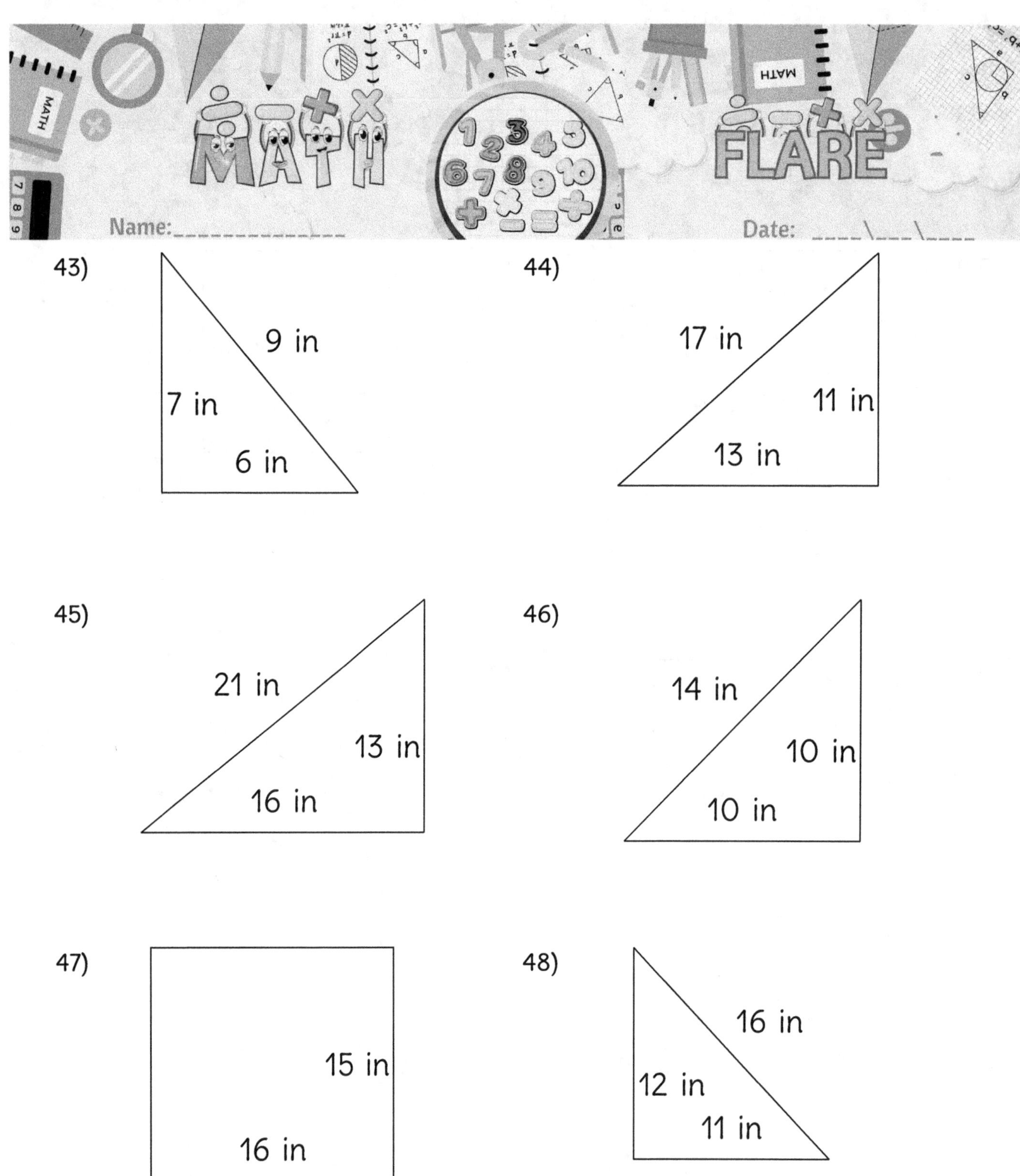

43)
9 in
7 in
6 in

44)
17 in
11 in
13 in

45)
21 in
13 in
16 in

46)
14 in
10 in
10 in

47)
15 in
16 in

48)
16 in
12 in
11 in

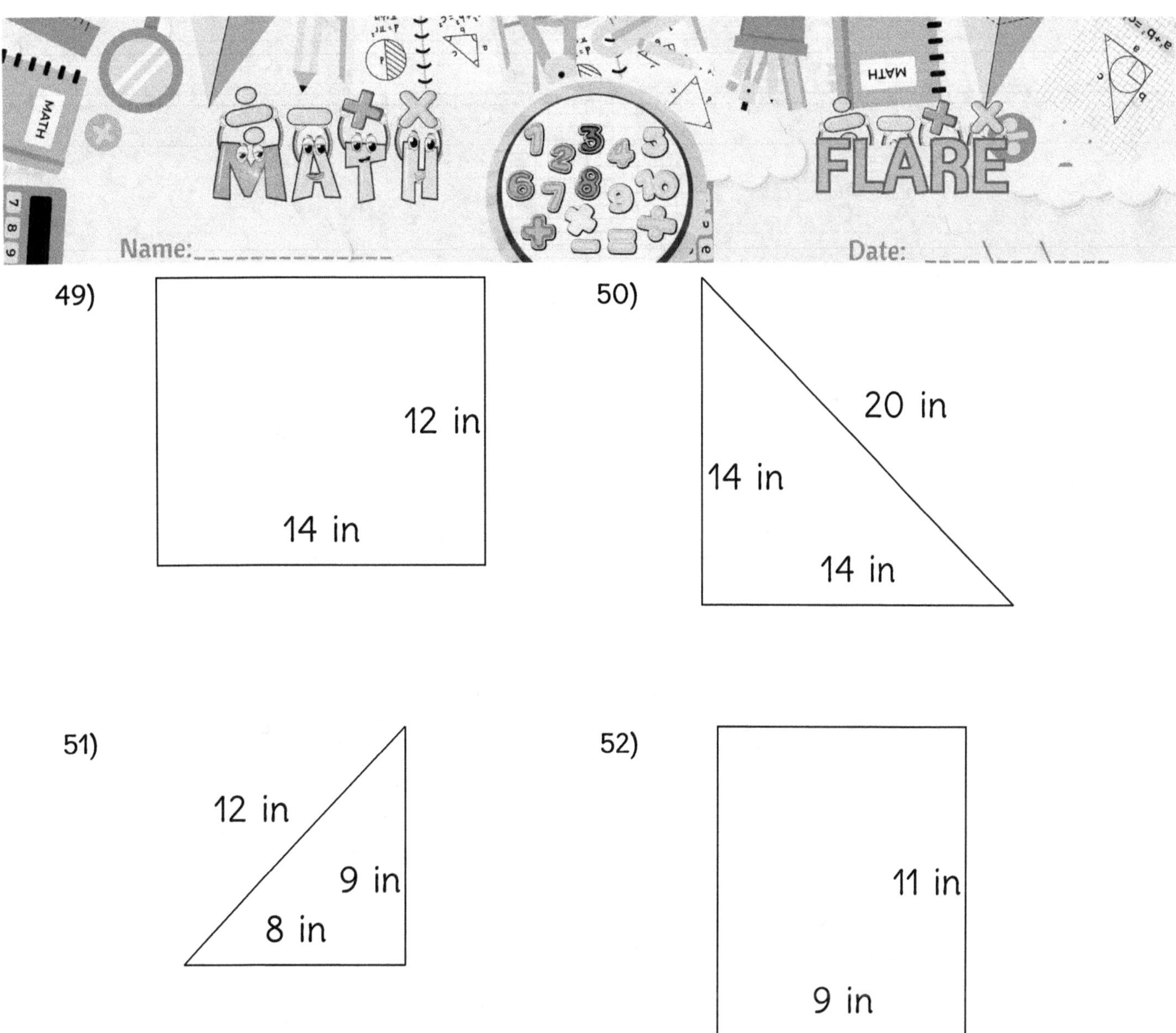

49)
12 in
14 in
50)
20 in
14 in
14 in
51)
12 in
9 in
8 in
52)
11 in
9 in

Name:________________   Date: _______________

53)
15 in
14 in

54)
16 in
12 in

55)
21 in
15 in
14 in

56)
10 in
7 in
7 in

57)
13 in
9 in
10 in

58)
10 in
7 in
7 in

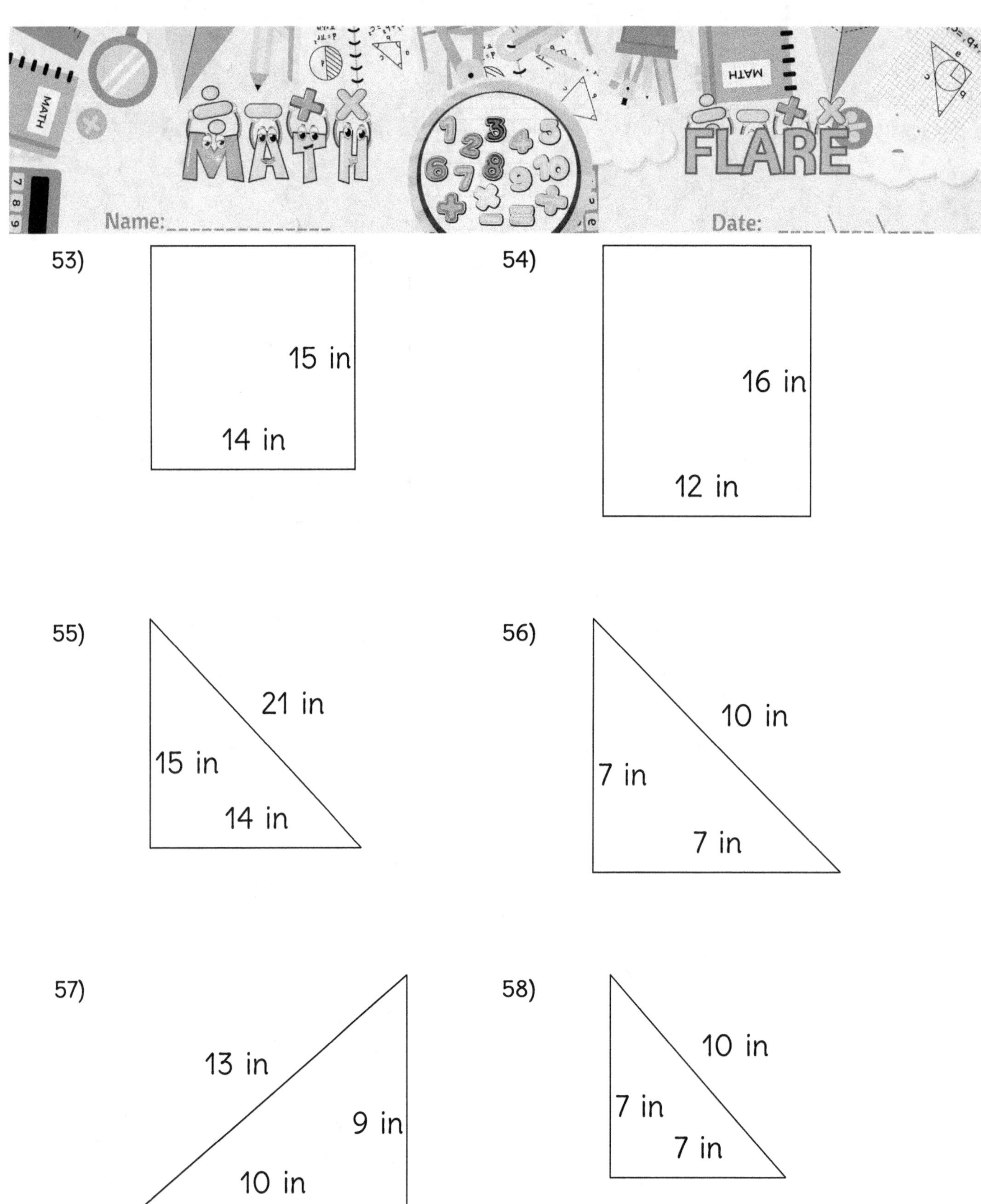

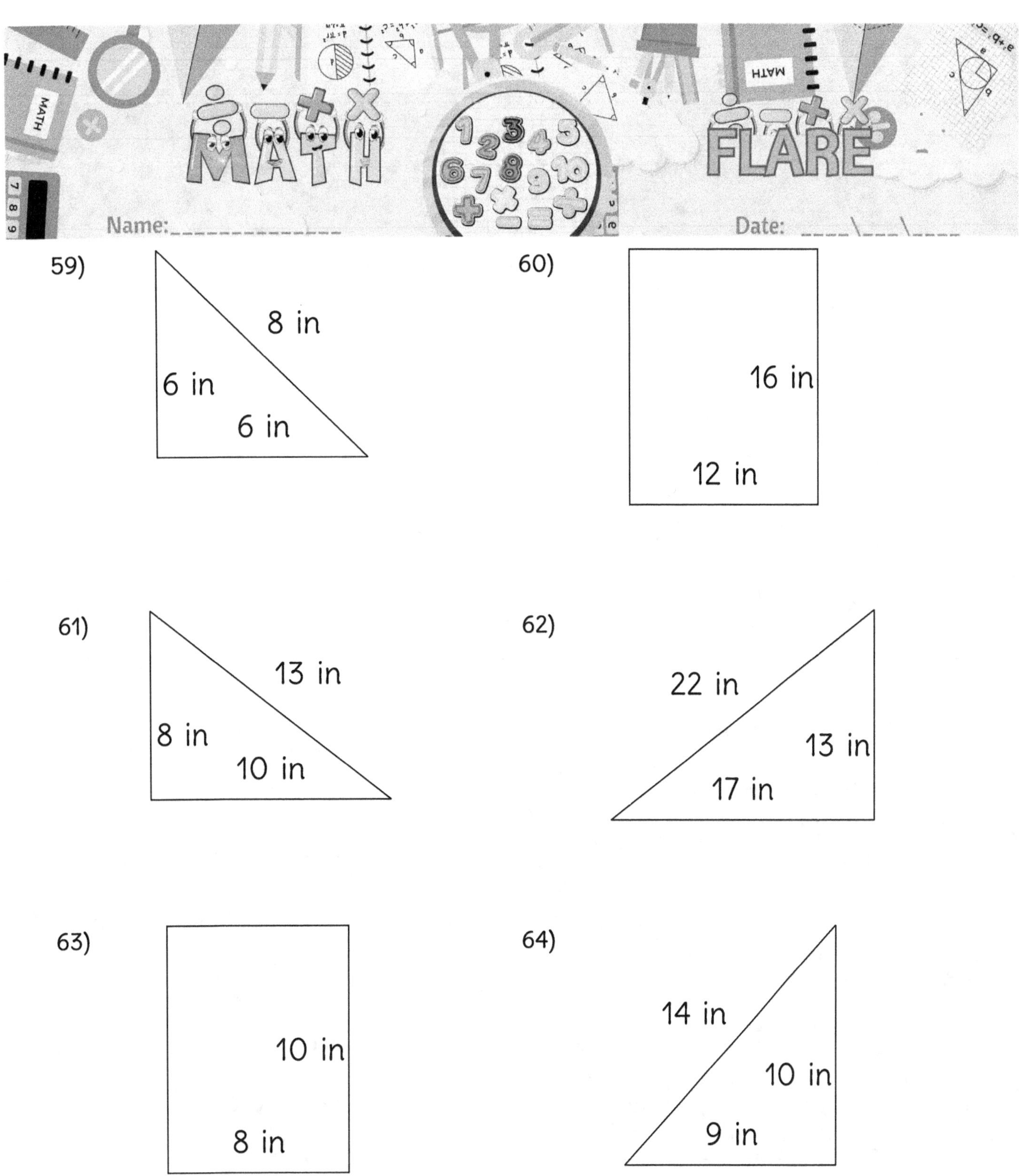

59)
8 in
6 in
6 in

60)
16 in
12 in

61)
13 in
8 in
10 in

62)
22 in
13 in
17 in

63)
10 in
8 in

64)
14 in
10 in
9 in

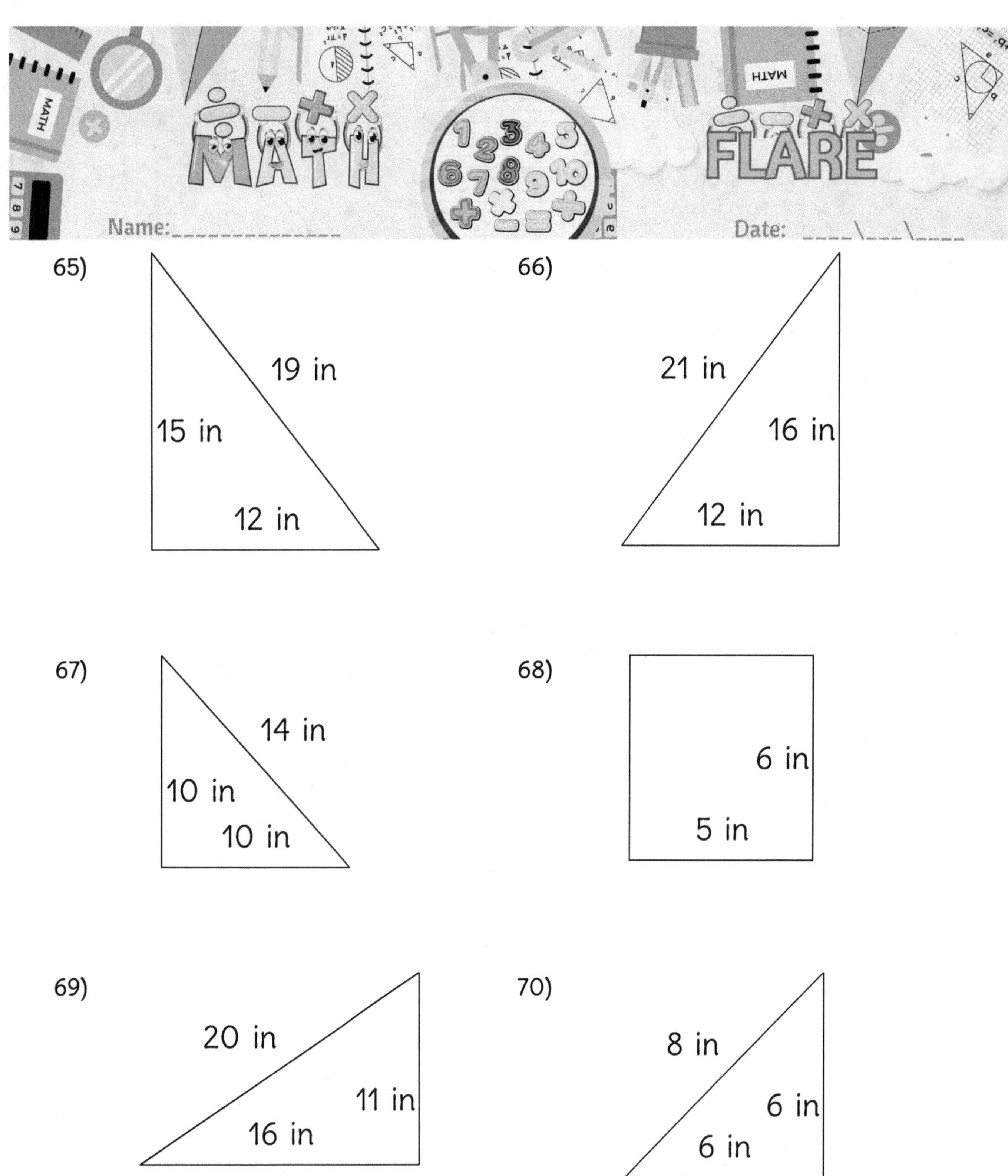

65)
19 in
15 in
12 in
66)
21 in
16 in
12 in
67)
14 in
10 in
10 in
68)
6 in
5 in
69)
20 in
11 in
16 in
70)
8 in
6 in
6 in

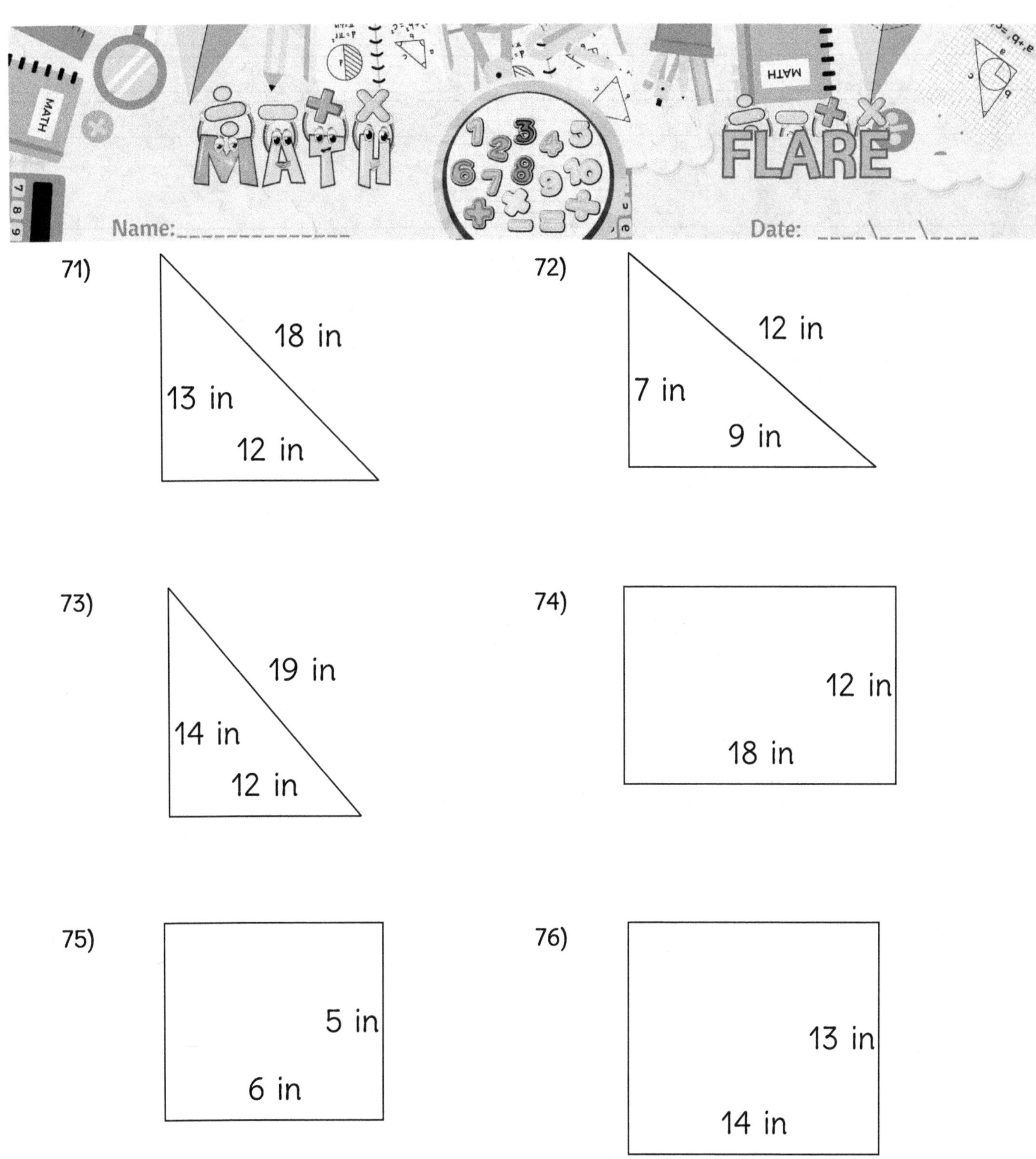
71)
18 in
13 in
12 in
72)
12 in
7 in
9 in
73)
19 in
14 in
12 in
74)
12 in
18 in
75)
5 in
6 in
76)
13 in
14 in

77)

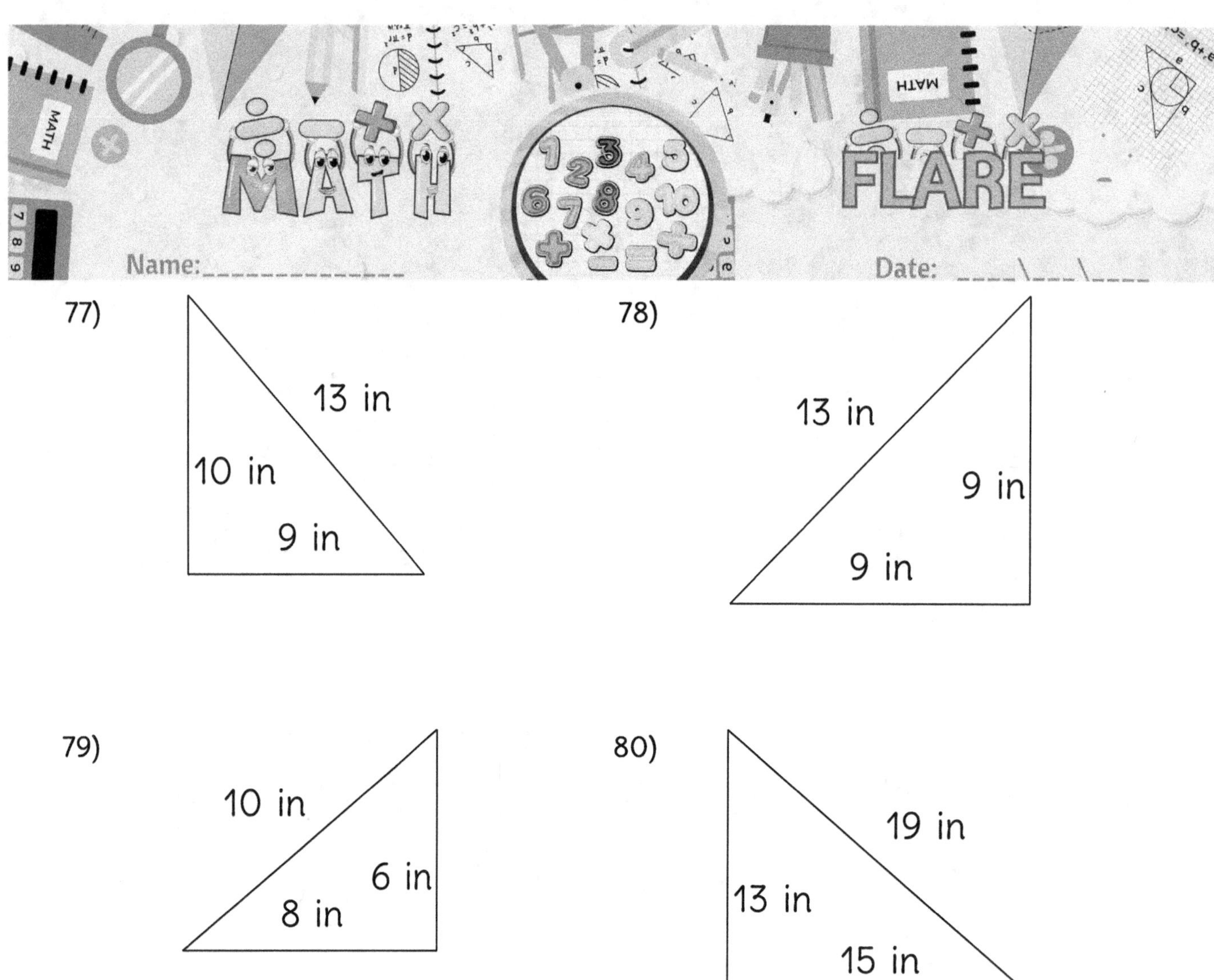

ANSWERS

Page 1: Addition with Regrouping

1. 1,252	2. 1,220	3. 1,510	4. 1,111	5. 1,123
6. 1,250	7. 771	8. 1,482	9. 1,224	10. 613
11. 1,110	12. 1,830	13. 1,935	14. 1,113	15. 1,510
16. 1,264	17. 1,372	18. 1,113	19. 1,142	20. 1,111
21. 1,176	22. 1,123	23. 1,210	24. 1,521	25. 1,710
26. 320	27. 1,811	28. 1,310	29. 1,124	30. 1,610
31. 1,522	32. 1,211	33. 1,170	34. 1,730	35. 1,331
36. 1,320	37. 424	38. 1,154	39. 1,396	40. 1,156
41. 1,114	42. 1,327	43. 1,113	44. 1,151	45. 251
46. 1,311	47. 1,721	48. 710	49. 1,361	50. 1,510
51. 1,212	52. 111	53. 1,320	54. 1,830	55. 1,260
56. 1,131	57. 1,110	58. 1,542	59. 1,431	60. 125
61. 1,111	62. 1,110	63. 833	64. 1,231	65. 1,110
66. 1,123	67. 1,231	68. 1,920	69. 1,461	70. 1,390
71. 1,150	72. 383	73. 1,110	74. 1,481	75. 571
76. 1,311	77. 1,122	78. 930	79. 1,212	80. 123
81. 1,152	82. 541	83. 1,640	84. 1,297	85. 1,150
86. 612	87. 1,333	88. 1,483	89. 1,240	90. 1,372
91. 314	92. 1,483	93. 1,113	94. 1,510	95. 533

96. 1,310	97. 1,713	98. 117	99. 1,251	100. 1,571
101. 1,141	102. 1,150	103. 1,110	104. 1,510	105. 1,330
106. 1,640	107. 1,365	108. 1,163	109. 1,520	110. 1,616
111. 1,160	112. 1,120	113. 1,121	114. 1,411	115. 764
116. 413	117. 1,013	118. 1,114	119. 1,140	120. 1,213
121. 1,113	122. 470	123. 1,512	124. 1,510	125. 520
126. 1,622	127. 1,541	128. 1,120	129. 1,230	130. 1,263
131. 1,211	132. 1,413	133. 1,210	134. 1,596	135. 1,263
136. 1,322	137. 610	138. 611	139. 1,424	140. 1,710
141. 1,216	142. 1,140	143. 1,437	144. 1,182	145. 1,723
146. 1,411	147. 121	148. 1,444	149. 1,650	150. 281
151. 1,310	152. 1,214	153. 113	154. 521	155. 224
156. 1,951	157. 1,540	158. 1,150	159. 1,114	160. 1,313
161. 1,110	162. 1,511	163. 322	164. 615	165. 1,711
166. 1,210	167. 1,441	168. 1,210	169. 1,130	170. 1,821
171. 1,226	172. 1,750	173. 1,736	174. 1,721	175. 1,270
176. 1,544	177. 1,061	178. 1,240	179. 1,691	180. 591
181. 1,326	182. 1,512	183. 220	184. 1,241	185. 1,750
186. 222	187. 1,511	188. 1,060	189. 1,230	190. 1,110
191. 1,215	192. 1,210	193. 1,336	194. 1,325	195. 1,334
196. 1,144	197. 1,642	198. 1,110	199. 124	200. 1,561

Page 11: Subtraction with Regrouping

1. 238	2. 58	3. 69	4. 23	5. 677	6. 436
7. 47	8. 86	9. 7	10. 289	11. 265	12. 68
13. 8	14. 104	15. 83	16. 159	17. 349	18. 19
19. 569	20. 169	21. 367	22. 287	23. 276	24. 76
25. 88	26. 79	27. 179	28. 85	29. 89	30. 468
31. 178	32. 4	33. 87	34. 344	35. 79	36. 288
37. 38	38. 77	39. 79	40. 59	41. 281	42. 286
43. 284	44. 15	45. 79	46. 87	47. 385	48. 189
49. 77	50. 56	51. 49	52. 687	53. 282	54. 79
55. 483	56. 168	57. 39	58. 89	59. 45	60. 88
61. 778	62. 57	63. 285	64. 6	65. 68	66. 79
67. 47	68. 79	69. 387	70. 379	71. 78	72. 27
73. 652	74. 248	75. 286	76. 77	77. 285	78. 459
79. 389	80. 372	81. 189	82. 29	83. 358	84. 789
85. 489	86. 59	87. 89	88. 29	89. 549	90. 688
91. 88	92. 69	93. 189	94. 136	95. 84	96. 74
97. 89	98. 879	99. 787	100. 89	101. 69	102. 59
103. 679	104. 169	105. 44	106. 264	107. 85	108. 288
109. 335	110. 381	111. 59	112. 38	113. 39	114. 89
115. 674	116. 139	117. 16	118. 586	119. 66	120. 688

121. 407   122. 589   123. 79   124. 443   125. 168   126. 78
127. 587   128. 4   129. 359   130. 88   131. 378   132. 776
133. 189   134. 79   135. 786   136. 279   137. 19   138. 477
139. 89   140. 47   141. 289   142. 86   143. 59   144. 7
145. 187   146. 87   147. 107   148. 278   149. 88   150. 69
151. 168   152. 86   153. 789   154. 477   155. 89   156. 88
157. 379   158. 69   159. 257   160. 24   161. 429   162. 288
163. 371   164. 59   165. 386   166. 186   167. 479   168. 86
169. 479   170. 137   171. 9   172. 166   173. 88   174. 168
175. 67   176. 89   177. 67   178. 131   179. 177   180. 58
181. 476   182. 387   183. 165   184. 58   185. 469   186. 49
187. 88   188. 67   189. 84   190. 286   191. 618   192. 57
193. 264   194. 27   195. 89   196. 85

Page 21: Addition Word Problems

1. 24   2. 25   3. 10   4. 30   5. 22   6. 32   7. 19   8. 15
9. 35   10. 23   11. 18   12. 12   13. 21   14. 23   15. 27   16. 27
17. 20   18. 26   19. 14   20. 23   21. 31   22. 31   23. 24   24. 29
25. 21   26. 34   27. 19   28. 12   29. 10   30. 21   31. 17   32. 24
33. 6   34. 14   35. 17   36. 38   37. 21   38. 5   39. 15   40. 24

Page 31: Subtraction Word Problems

1. 0   2. 2   3. 1   4. 4   5. 0   6. 0   7. 3   8. 0   9. 0   10. 0

11. 2   12. 0   13. 5   14. 3   15. 0   16. 3   17. 2   18. 0   19. 0   20. 3

21. 3   22. 2   23. 3   24. 1   25. 0   26. 5   27. 4   28. 4   29. 2   30. 1

31. 5   32. 3   33. 6   34. 0   35. 5   36. 1   37. 6   38. 1   39. 0   40. 5

41. 7   42. 0   43. 7   44. 0

Page 42:   Multiplication by 1

1. 5   2. 1   3. 6   4. 3   5. 8   6. 4   7. 2   8. 9   9. 7   10. 3

11. 8   12. 6   13. 7   14. 9   15. 4   16. 5   17. 2   18. 8   19. 4   20. 5

Page 43:   Multiplication by 2

1. 4   2. 10   3. 8   4. 6   5. 12   6. 18   7. 2   8. 16   9. 14

10. 16   11. 10   12. 6   13. 14   14. 8   15. 2   16. 18   17. 12   18. 8

19. 2   20. 6

Page 44:   Multiplication by 3

1. 18   2. 9   3. 24   4. 27   5. 21   6. 6   7. 12   8. 15   9. 3

10. 6   11. 12   12. 15   13. 24   14. 21   15. 18   16. 27   17. 3   18. 9

19. 18   20. 18

Page 45:   Multiplication by 4

1. 24   2. 12   3. 20   4. 28   5. 8   6. 4   7. 16   8. 36

9. 32   10. 8   11. 20   12. 32   13. 24   14. 12   15. 28   16. 4

17. 36   18. 24   19. 20   20. 24

Page 46:   Multiplication by 5

1. 20   2. 15   3. 10   4. 25   5. 5   6. 30   7. 35   8. 40   9. 45

10. 35   11. 20   12. 30   13. 15   14. 40   15. 45   16. 5   17. 10   18. 15

19. 40   20. 10

Page 47: Multiplication by 6

1. 12	2. 48	3. 54	4. 42	5. 6	6. 30	7. 36	8. 18
9. 24	10. 42	11. 24	12. 48	13. 18	14. 30	15. 6	16. 12
17. 54	18. 24	19. 36	20. 30				

Page 48: Multiplication by 7

1. 35	2. 49	3. 7	4. 28	5. 42	6. 14	7. 56	8. 21
9. 63	10. 14	11. 28	12. 35	13. 56	14. 7	15. 63	16. 21
17. 42	18. 28	19. 49	20. 49				

Page 49: Multiplication by 8

1. 8	2. 64	3. 48	4. 16	5. 56	6. 72	7. 32	8. 40
9. 24	10. 8	11. 32	12. 40	13. 56	14. 16	15. 72	16. 48
17. 24	18. 40	19. 72	20. 40				

Page 50: Multiplication by 9

1. 63	2. 72	3. 54	4. 18	5. 45	6. 9	7. 81	8. 27
9. 36	10. 18	11. 36	12. 45	13. 27	14. 72	15. 54	16. 63
17. 9	18. 27	19. 45	20. 63				

Page 51: Multiplication by 10

1. 70	2. 30	3. 20	4. 80	5. 90	6. 60	7. 50	8. 10
9. 40	10. 70	11. 50	12. 10	13. 30	14. 60	15. 20	16. 80
17. 40	18. 90	19. 30	20. 60				

Page 52: Multiplication

1. 56	2. 21	3. 12	4. 10	5. 9	6. 50	7. 18
8. 16	9. 28	10. 24	11. 81	12. 36	13. 35	14. 12
15. 14	16. 36	17. 6	18. 40	19. 45	20. 63	21. 10
22. 25	23. 36	24. 7	25. 24	26. 64	27. 40	28. 54
29. 80	30. 48	31. 30	32. 4	33. 18	34. 15	35. 18
36. 60	37. 16	38. 72	39. 42	40. 21	41. 10	42. 60
43. 27	44. 30	45. 8	46. 6	47. 27	48. 14	49. 42
50. 32	51. 63	52. 40	53. 10	54. 12	55. 16	56. 54
57. 4	58. 90	59. 45	60. 9	61. 1	62. 30	63. 20
64. 90	65. 20	66. 80	67. 32	68. 4	69. 18	70. 56
71. 6	72. 70	73. 24	74. 5	75. 40	76. 8	77. 8
78. 20	79. 15	80. 70	81. 30	82. 12	83. 6	84. 72
85. 24	86. 35	87. 49	88. 8	89. 48	90. 2	91. 9
92. 28	93. 20	94. 50	95. 7	96. 100	97. 3	98. 3
99. 2	100. 5					

Page 57: Multiplication: 2 x 1

1. 80	2. 84	3. 88	4. 63	5. 86	6. 61	7. 39
8. 62	9. 42	10. 48	11. 99	12. 60	13. 26	14. 46
15. 55	16. 66	17. 68	18. 69	19. 12	20. 68	21. 33
22. 40	23. 93	24. 25	25. 40	26. 96	27. 90	28. 44

29. 50 30. 98 31. 36 32. 44 33. 48 34. 28 35. 80

36. 78 37. 55 38. 88 39. 86 40. 54 41. 60 42. 30

43. 84 44. 82 45. 66 46. 52 47. 22 48. 64 49. 18

50. 91 51. 24 52. 35 53. 47 54. 11 55. 67 56. 88

57. 20 58. 20 59. 56 60. 69 61. 15 62. 44 63. 89

64. 77 65. 57 66. 26 67. 43 68. 59 69. 50 70. 32

71. 92 72. 39 73. 70 74. 81 75. 42 76. 19 77. 71

78. 72 79. 17 80. 66 81. 53 82. 34 83. 46 84. 85

85. 13 86. 30 87. 95 88. 74 89. 37 90. 96 91. 97

92. 64 93. 93 94. 58 95. 75 96. 87 97. 45 98. 94

99. 16 100. 22

Page 62: Commutative Property

1. 7 2. 7 3. 8 4. 4 5. 9 6. 4 7. 9 8. 2 9. 7

10. 4 11. 4 12. 8 13. 5 14. 9 15. 3 16. 3 17. 4 18. 7

19. 1 20. 3 21. 7 22. 4 23. 5 24. 3 25. 7 26. 9 27. 8

28. 7 29. 7 30. 5 31. 8 32. 1 33. 3 34. 10 35. 9 36. 6

37. 2 38. 5 39. 6 40. 8 41. 9 42. 2 43. 3 44. 7 45. 1

46. 5 47. 6 48. 6 49. 6 50. 7 51. 2 52. 1

Page 65: Division by 2

1. 5 2. 18 3. 12 4. 14 5. 1 6. 3 7. 11 8. 16 9. 17

10. 4 11. 2 12. 6 13. 9 14. 7 15. 13 16. 19

Page 66:   Division by 3

1. 2   2. 10   3. 6   4. 3   5. 9   6. 8   7. 1   8. 5   9. 7   10. 4

11. 2   12. 3   13. 7   14. 3   15. 7   16. 9   17. 9   18. 9   19. 2   20. 7

Page 67:   Division by 4

1. 9   2. 2   3. 5   4. 4   5. 8   6. 7   7. 3   8. 10   9. 6   10. 1

11. 7   12. 8   13. 4   14. 9   15. 4   16. 7   17. 9   18. 5   19. 2   20. 4

Page 68:   Division by 5

1. 7   2. 6   3. 5   4. 2   5. 4   6. 10   7. 3   8. 9   9. 8

10. 1   11. 3   12. 9   13. 6   14. 3   15. 9   16. 6   17. 10   18. 2

19. 7   20. 6

Page 69:   Division by 6

1. 3   2. 6   3. 10   4. 5   5. 2   6. 7   7. 1   8. 8   9. 4   10. 9

11. 6   12. 2   13. 7   14. 3   15. 9   16. 5   17. 9   18. 9   19. 2   20. 5

Page 70:   Division by 7

1. 4   2. 8   3. 7   4. 9   5. 6   6. 10   7. 5   8. 3   9. 1   10. 2

11. 7   12. 7   13. 9   14. 6   15. 5   16. 2   17. 5   18. 6   19. 5   20. 3

Page 71:   Division by 8

1. 5   2. 1   3. 4   4. 8   5. 10   6. 9   7. 7   8. 2   9. 3   10. 6

11. 5   12. 8   13. 3   14. 1   15. 7   16. 2   17. 2   18. 7   19. 7   20. 3

Page 72:   Division by 9

1. 9   2. 2   3. 6   4. 8   5. 1   6. 5   7. 3   8. 4   9. 7

10. 10   11. 8   12. 8   13. 2   14. 2   15. 7   16. 3   17. 2   18. 2

19. 3   20. 5

Page 73: Division by 10

1. 10   2. 5   3. 3   4. 11   5. 7   6. 16   7. 1   8. 17   9. 15

10. 12   11. 20   12. 8   13. 6   14. 9   15. 18

Page 74: Basic Division

1. 6   2. 11   3. 11   4. 5   5. 20   6. 19   7. 7

8. 9   9. 13   10. 17   11. 10   12. 18   13. 2   14. 9

15. 3   16. 11   17. 5   18. 1   19. 15   20. 12   21. 12

22. 11   23. 19   24. 5   25. 4   26. 14   27. 13   28. 5

29. 2   30. 2   31. 6   32. 8   33. 19   34. 8   35. 18

36. 7   37. 17   38. 16   39. 7   40. 15   41. 4   42. 3

43. 9   44. 10   45. 17   46. 7   47. 19   48. 3   49. 12

50. 14   51. 11   52. 20   53. 7   54. 9   55. 5   56. 3

57. 3   58. 13   59. 1   60. 19   61. 9   62. 6   63. 2

64. 10   65. 17   66. 16   67. 12   68. 17   69. 5   70. 20

71. 11   72. 6   73. 10   74. 10   75. 14   76. 17   77. 12

78. 8   79. 13   80. 19   81. 7   82. 18   83. 8   84. 11

85. 14   86. 8   87. 17   88. 6   89. 7   90. 13   91. 18

92. 16   93. 6   94. 4   95. 6   96. 17   97. 7   98. 19

99. 11   100. 11   101. 16   102. 9   103. 10   104. 10   105. 19

106. 13   107. 20   108. 15   109. 2   110. 18   111. 16   112. 15

113. 16   114. 12   115. 16   116. 8   117. 20   118. 2   119. 13

120. 9

Page 80: Place Value

1. 5 thousands

2. 0 tens

3. 1 one

4. 3 hundreds

5. 7 thousands

6. 3 ones

7. 7 hundreds

8. 1 hundred

9. 2 ten thousands

10. 8 ten thousands

11. 5 tens

12. 5 tens

13. 2 tens

14. 5 tens

15. 1 ten thousand

16. 9 ones

17. 0 ones

18. 8 thousands

19. 7 hundreds

20. 7 hundreds

21. 9 hundreds

22. 4 ones

23. 1 one

24. 9 ones

25. 4 ten thousands

26. 0 tens

27. 4 ten thousands

28. 4 ones

29. 1 thousand

30. 4 hundreds

31. 8 ten thousands

32. 7 ten thousands

33. 8 ones

34. 7 ones

35. 2 ten thousands

36. 5 ten thousands

37. 5 ten thousands

38. 4 thousands

39. 4 hundreds

40. 7 hundreds

41. 6 hundreds

42. 2 ones

43. 5 ten thousands

44. 6 hundreds

45. 3 thousands

46. 6 tens

47. 5 tens

48. 7 ten thousands

49. 6 ten thousands

50. 7 thousands

51. 0 hundreds

52. 3 thousands

53. 6 ten thousands

54. 8 tens

55. 8 tens 56. 0 ones 57. 2 ten thousands

58. 7 tens 59. 4 thousands 60. 0 hundreds

61. 5 hundreds 62. 9 hundreds 63. 6 ones

64. 4 tens 65. 8 tens 66. 2 tens

67. 9 thousands 68. 1 one 69. 5 ten thousands

70. 8 ones 71. 9 ones 72. 7 tens

73. 2 hundreds 74. 2 thousands 75. 2 ones

76. 4 ones 77. 4 ones 78. 2 hundreds

79. 0 thousands 80. 1 hundred 81. 2 thousands

82. 4 thousands 83. 9 thousands 84. 1 ten

85. 1 ten 86. 2 hundreds 87. 4 ones

88. 2 ten thousands 89. 3 ones 90. 0 ones

91. 2 hundreds 92. 9 ones 93. 8 tens

94. 4 thousands

Page 86: Place Value: Expanded Notation

1. 63,698 2. 40,139 3. 19,267 4. 99,690 5. 17,274

6. 29,809 7. 57,758 8. 14,996 9. 86,503 10. 84,168

11. 90,306 12. 71,850 13. 66,410 14. 27,529 15. 31,439

16. 52,329 17. 46,057 18. 32,760 19. 94,411 20. 20,665

21. 78,887 22. 64,790 23. 23,839 24. 29,458 25. 32,063

26. 52,610 27. 56,247 28. 95,481 29. 49,929 30. 42,318

31. 34,221   32. 44,724   33. 28,058   34. 66,394   35. 77,316

36. 37,611   37. 29,325   38. 41,547   39. 54,181   40. 13,771

41. 74,493   42. 21,221   43. 59,827   44. 99,631   45. 85,561

46. 84,025   47. 35,071   48. 85,041   49. 29,004   50. 54,053

51. 59,070   52. 42,265   53. 12,054   54. 67,744   55. 57,774

56. 98,907   57. 26,301   58. 89,808   59. 77,628   60. 64,663

61. 73,560   62. 62,276   63. 65,066   64. 54,184   65. 59,946

66. 55,581   67. 53,792   68. 10,016   69. 50,212   70. 93,827

71. 33,003   72. 14,510   73. 78,578   74. 90,640   75. 46,171

76. 67,667   77. 14,962   78. 24,207   79. 43,896   80. 48,037

81. 27,539   82. 71,206   83. 76,477   84. 95,875   85. 83,247

86. 91,955   87. 42,670   88. 60,314   89. 18,620   90. 78,408

91. 21,311   92. 39,516   93. 63,918   94. 89,517   95. 40,210

96. 22,218   97. 56,154

Page 100: Place Value: Expanded Notation

1. 1 ten thousand + 5 thousands + 6 hundreds + 4 tens + 3 ones

2. 4 ten thousands + 9 thousands + 6 hundreds + 8 tens + 4 ones

3. 3 ten thousands + 9 thousands + 9 hundreds + 8 tens

4. 4 ten thousands + 2 hundreds + 3 tens + 3 ones

5. 3 ten thousands + 5 thousands + 5 tens + 5 ones

6. 4 ten thousands + 4 thousands + 8 hundreds + 2 tens + 9 ones

7. 3 ten thousands + 5 thousands + 1 hundred + 7 tens + 6 ones

8. 3 ten thousands + 1 thousand + 5 tens

9. 5 ten thousands + 4 thousands + 5 hundreds + 6 tens

10. 6 ten thousands + 3 thousands + 6 hundreds + 8 tens + 6 ones

11. 2 ten thousands + 1 thousand + 4 hundreds + 1 ten + 3 ones

12. 3 ten thousands + 1 thousand + 5 hundreds + 7 tens + 3 ones

13. 9 ten thousands + 1 hundred + 6 ones

14. 9 ten thousands + 3 thousands + 9 hundreds + 4 tens + 4 ones

15. 1 ten thousand + 2 thousands + 9 tens + 3 ones

16. 5 ten thousands + 5 thousands + 9 hundreds + 1 ten + 2 ones

17. 3 ten thousands + 9 thousands + 5 hundreds + 9 tens + 1 one

18. 4 ten thousands + 7 thousands + 1 hundred + 2 tens + 4 ones

19. 1 ten thousand + 2 thousands + 3 hundreds + 5 tens + 5 ones

20. 8 ten thousands + 5 thousands + 7 hundreds + 9 tens + 8 ones

21. 6 ten thousands + 9 thousands + 1 hundred + 8 tens + 9 ones

22. 7 ten thousands + 9 hundreds + 3 tens + 6 ones

23. 6 ten thousands + 7 thousands + 9 hundreds + 9 tens + 1 one

24. 2 ten thousands + 2 thousands + 9 hundreds + 1 ten + 1 one

25. 9 ten thousands + 3 thousands + 4 hundreds + 7 tens + 7 ones

26. 9 ten thousands + 1 thousand + 3 hundreds + 9 tens + 5 ones

27. 7 ten thousands + 1 thousand + 8 hundreds + 3 ones

28. 8 ten thousands + 2 thousands + 5 hundreds + 1 ten + 6 ones

29. 9 ten thousands + 3 thousands + 4 hundreds + 8 tens + 6 ones

30. 5 ten thousands + 5 hundreds + 9 tens

31. 8 ten thousands + 9 thousands + 6 tens + 1 one

32. 6 ten thousands + 4 hundreds + 3 tens

33. 3 ten thousands + 3 thousands + 9 hundreds + 5 tens + 3 ones

34. 2 ten thousands + 1 thousand + 5 hundreds + 1 ten + 2 ones

35. 9 ten thousands + 9 thousands + 3 hundreds + 1 ten + 8 ones

36. 7 ten thousands + 4 thousands + 5 hundreds + 2 tens + 2 ones

37. 1 ten thousand + 3 thousands + 9 hundreds + 1 ten + 6 ones

38. 1 ten thousand + 7 thousands + 8 hundreds + 4 ones

39. 9 ten thousands + 2 thousands + 4 hundreds + 8 tens + 3 ones

40. 3 ten thousands + 6 thousands + 3 hundreds + 7 tens + 7 ones

41. 5 ten thousands + 1 thousand + 3 hundreds + 1 one

42. 7 ten thousands + 4 thousands + 8 hundreds + 2 tens + 6 ones

43. 3 ten thousands + 8 thousands + 6 hundreds + 8 tens + 7 ones

44. 3 ten thousands + 8 thousands + 2 hundreds + 6 tens + 9 ones

45. 3 ten thousands + 1 thousand + 2 hundreds + 5 tens + 7 ones

46. 3 ten thousands + 8 thousands + 7 hundreds + 4 tens + 1 one

47. 2 ten thousands + 8 thousands + 5 hundreds + 1 ten + 3 ones

48. 8 ten thousands + 4 thousands + 4 hundreds + 6 tens + 3 ones

49. 1 ten thousand + 9 thousands + 2 hundreds + 1 ten + 7 ones

50. 8 ten thousands + 3 thousands + 6 hundreds + 3 ones

51. 3 ten thousands + 4 thousands + 3 hundreds + 2 tens + 8 ones

52. 5 ten thousands + 2 thousands + 3 hundreds + 9 tens + 2 ones

53. 3 ten thousands + 7 thousands + 8 hundreds + 5 tens + 5 ones

54. 3 ten thousands + 6 thousands + 4 hundreds + 1 ten + 9 ones

55. 8 ten thousands + 6 thousands + 9 hundreds + 6 tens + 4 ones

56. 4 ten thousands + 4 thousands + 7 hundreds + 6 ones

57. 8 ten thousands + 1 thousand + 6 hundreds + 9 tens + 3 ones

58. 2 ten thousands + 7 thousands + 6 tens + 9 ones

59. 4 ten thousands + 6 thousands + 7 hundreds + 5 tens + 5 ones

60. 4 ten thousands + 3 thousands + 6 hundreds + 5 tens + 9 ones

61. 7 ten thousands + 3 thousands + 2 tens + 5 ones

62. 5 ten thousands + 2 thousands + 6 hundreds + 5 tens + 9 ones

63. 3 ten thousands + 7 thousands + 5 hundreds + 6 tens + 2 ones

64. 1 ten thousand + 3 thousands + 9 hundreds + 7 tens

65. 7 ten thousands + 4 thousands + 6 hundreds + 2 tens + 5 ones

66. 6 ten thousands + 9 hundreds + 8 tens + 2 ones

67. 9 ten thousands + 7 thousands + 6 hundreds + 1 ten + 8 ones

68. 7 ten thousands + 8 thousands + 5 hundreds + 9 tens + 4 ones

69. 9 ten thousands + 4 thousands + 6 hundreds + 2 tens + 5 ones

70. 3 ten thousands + 7 thousands + 5 hundreds + 7 tens + 1 one

71. 5 ten thousands + 1 thousand + 9 hundreds + 9 tens + 5 ones

72. 3 ten thousands + 1 thousand + 7 hundreds + 8 tens + 7 ones

73. 5 ten thousands + 4 thousands + 6 hundreds + 4 tens

74. 7 ten thousands + 5 thousands + 9 hundreds + 7 tens + 7 ones

75. 4 ten thousands + 4 thousands + 4 hundreds + 9 tens + 7 ones

76. 9 ten thousands + 4 thousands + 3 hundreds + 6 tens + 3 ones

77. 4 ten thousands + 2 thousands + 2 hundreds + 4 tens + 9 ones

78. 3 ten thousands + 9 thousands + 7 hundreds + 2 tens + 2 ones

79. 9 ten thousands + 1 thousand + 6 hundreds + 5 tens + 3 ones

80. 6 ten thousands + 4 thousands + 7 hundreds + 3 tens + 5 ones

81. 7 ten thousands + 2 thousands + 8 hundreds + 8 tens + 2 ones

82. 8 ten thousands + 7 thousands + 3 hundreds + 3 tens + 9 ones

83. 7 ten thousands + 3 thousands + 2 hundreds + 9 tens + 9 ones

84. 1 ten thousand + 9 thousands + 8 hundreds + 8 tens + 3 ones

85. 2 ten thousands + 6 thousands + 2 hundreds + 6 tens + 3 ones

86. 4 ten thousands + 6 thousands + 6 hundreds + 6 tens + 8 ones

87. 3 ten thousands + 2 thousands + 5 hundreds + 7 tens + 6 ones

88. 9 ten thousands + 7 thousands + 5 hundreds + 3 tens + 3 ones

89. 3 ten thousands + 4 thousands + 5 hundreds + 4 tens + 7 ones

Page 115: Place Value: Expanded Notation

1. 64,612
2. 92,828
3. 86,847
4. 71,047
5. 58,824

6. 63,350
7. 98,641
8. 47,263
9. 34,717
10. 63,643

11. 70,274
12. 41,122
13. 49,918
14. 89,837
15. 81,646

16. 41,608
17. 12,540
18. 97,751
19. 61,877
20. 91,921

21. 92,600
22. 12,458
23. 51,971
24. 35,414
25. 82,019

26. 70,775
27. 85,685
28. 79,359
29. 27,680
30. 87,706

31. 37,956
32. 38,406
33. 10,085
34. 54,046
35. 40,013

36. 44,741
37. 65,148
38. 60,739
39. 95,815
40. 22,627

41. 45,855
42. 57,100
43. 17,531
44. 76,078
45. 31,379

46. 33,613
47. 32,964
48. 97,502
49. 91,652
50. 78,274

51. 23,722
52. 48,916
53. 70,698
54. 15,612
55. 41,947

56. 62,154
57. 50,858
58. 61,433
59. 89,027
60. 88,048

61. 77,665
62. 29,281
63. 29,583
64. 47,010
65. 35,687

66. 41,868
67. 41,037
68. 95,871
69. 59,824
70. 46,905

71. 76,460
72. 51,801
73. 11,936
74. 49,250
75. 56,066

76. 45,500
77. 94,925
78. 75,892
79. 14,035
80. 58,406

81. 47,811
82. 88,182
83. 49,405
84. 73,984
85. 89,040

86. 67,707
87. 94,472

Page 126: Understanding Time

1. 

What time will it be in 3 hours 8 minutes 14 seconds?

2. 

What time will it be in 9 hours 20 minutes 46 seconds?

3. 

What time was it 8 hours 50 minutes 1 second ago?

4. 

What time will it be in 10 hours 8 minutes 43 seconds?

5. 

What time will it be in 9 hours 56 minutes 41 seconds?

6. 

What time will it be in 7 hours 13 minutes 18 seconds?

7. 

What time was it 10 hours 24 minutes 3 seconds ago?

8. 

What time will it be in 5 hours 29 minutes 29 seconds?

9. 

What time will it be in 11 hours 22 minutes 0 seconds?

10. 

What time was it 9 hours 1 minute 24 seconds ago?

11. 

What time will it be in 5 hours 2 minutes 37 seconds?

12. 

What time will it be in 2 hours 2 minutes 44 seconds?

13. 

What time was it 1 hour 16 minutes 27 seconds ago?

14. 

What time was it 2 hours 35 minutes 50 seconds ago?

15. 

What time will it be in 1 hour 5 minutes 22 seconds?

16. 

What time will it be in 2 hours 1 minute 26 seconds?

17.

What time will it be in 2 hours 52 minutes 20 seconds?

18. 

What time will it be in 4 hours 45 minutes 44 seconds?

19. 

What time was it 5 hours 17 minutes 26 seconds ago?

20. 

What time will it be in 11 hours 4 minutes 56 seconds?

21. 

What time was it 2 hours 51 minutes 15 seconds ago?

22. 

What time will it be in 6 hours 59 minutes 43 seconds?

23. 

What time will it be in 2 hours 42 minutes 20 seconds?

24. 

What time was it 10 hours 43 minutes 44 seconds ago?

25. 

What time will it be in 11 hours 12 minutes 48 seconds?

26. 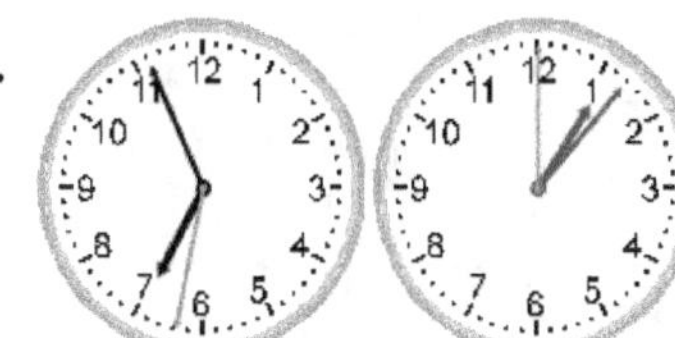

What time will it be in 6 hours 11 minutes 53 seconds?

27. 

What time was it 4 hours 53 minutes 17 seconds ago?

28. 

What time was it 3 hours 49 minutes 21 seconds ago?

29. 

What time was it 7 hours 16 minutes 8 seconds ago?

30. 

What time will it be in 10 hours 33 minutes 47 seconds?

31. 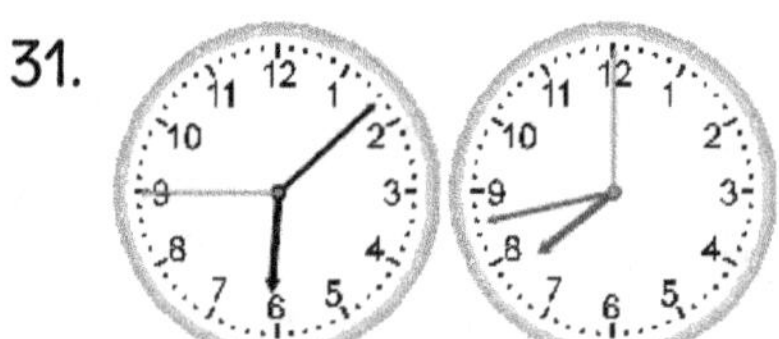

What time will it be in 1 hour 35 minutes 30 seconds?

32. 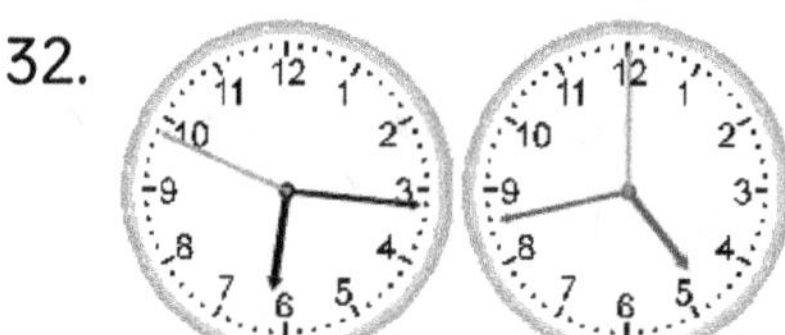

What time was it 1 hour 33 minutes 49 seconds ago?

33. 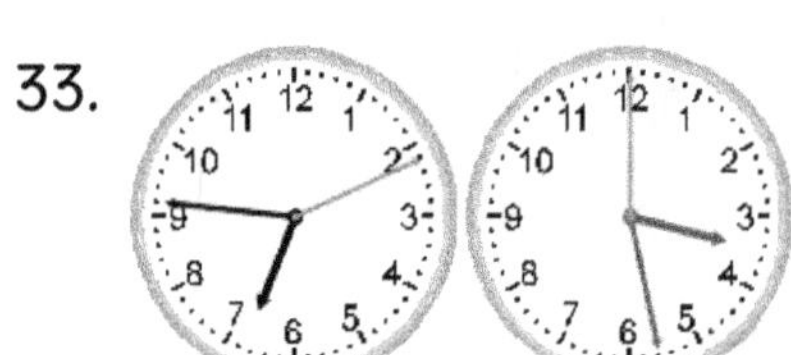

What time will it be in 8 hours 42 minutes 22 seconds?

34. 

What time will it be in 4 hours 53 minutes 55 seconds?

35. 

What time was it 5 hours 25 minutes 19 seconds ago?

36. 

What time will it be in 3 hours 13 minutes 14 seconds?

37. 

What time was it 3 hours 32 minutes 42 seconds ago?

38. 

What time was it 3 hours 12 minutes 51 seconds ago?

39. 

What time was it 3 hours 44 minutes 41 seconds ago?

40. 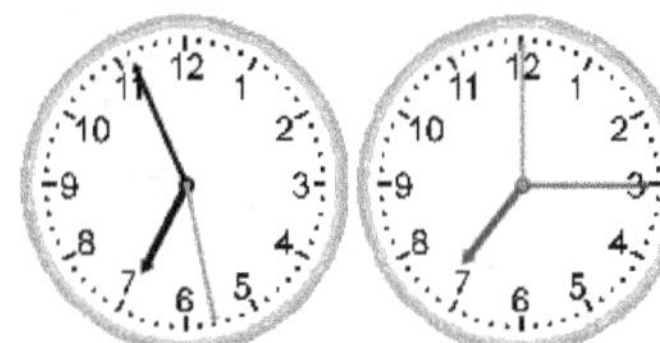

What time was it 11 hours 41 minutes 8 seconds ago?

Page 136: Area and Perimeter: Rectangles and Triangles

1. P=51 A=112.5
2. P=34 A=72
3. P=34 A=50
4. P=56 A=133
5. P=58 A=144
6. P=53 A=114
7. P=21 A=17.5
8. P=56 A=187
9. P=60 A=221
10. P=57 A=135
11. P=19 A=15
12. P=44 A=120
13. P=38 A=90
14. P=17 A=12.5
15. P=26 A=42
16. P=31 A=40.5
17. P=38 A=60
18. P=24 A=24
19. P=54 A=180
20. P=56 A=195
21. P=49 A=105
22. P=28 A=49
23. P=41 A=72
24. P=45 A=84
25. P=52 A=112
26. P=60 A=224
27. P=26 A=42
28. P=27 A=32
29. P=56 A=187
30. P=28 A=49
31. P=60 A=216
32. P=27 A=32
33. P=24 A=24
34. P=48 A=143
35. P=34 A=49.5
36. P=56 A=196

37. P=32 A=64

38. P=39 A=65

39. P=26 A=40

40. P=34 A=72

41. P=52 A=168

42. P=29 A=36

43. P=22 A=21

44. P=41 A=71.5

45. P=50 A=104

46. P=34 A=50

47. P=62 A=240

48. P=39 A=66

49. P=52 A=168

50. P=48 A=98

51. P=29 A=36

52. P=40 A=99

53. P=58 A=210

54. P=56 A=192

55. P=50 A=105

56. P=24 A=24.5

57. P=32 A=45

58. P=24 A=24.5

59. P=20 A=18

60. P=56 A=192

61. P=31 A=40

62. P=52 A=110.5

63. P=36 A=80

64. P=33 A=45

65. P=46 A=90

66. P=49 A=96

67. P=34 A=50

68. P=22 A=30

69. P=47 A=88

70. P=20 A=18

71. P=43 A=78

72. P=28 A=31.5

73. P=45 A=84

74. P=60 A=216

75. P=22 A=30

76. P=54 A=182

77. P=32 A=45

78. P=31 A=40.5

79. P=24 A=24

80. P=47 A=97.5